A narrative of the life of Mrs. Charlotte Charke, (youngest daughter of Colley Cibber, Esq;) ... written by herself.

Charlotte Charke

A narrative of the life of Mrs. Charlotte Charke, (youngest daughter of Colley Cibber, Esq;) ... written by herself.
Charke, Charlotte
ESTCID: T068299
Reproduction from British Library
With a half-title.
London : printed for W. Reeve; A. Dodd; E. Cook, 1755.
[2],277,[1]p.,plate : port. ; 12°

Eighteenth Century
Collections Online
Print Editions

Gale ECCO Print Editions

Relive history with *Eighteenth Century Collections Online*, now available in print for the independent historian and collector. This series includes the most significant English-language and foreign-language works printed in Great Britain during the eighteenth century, and is organized in seven different subject areas including literature and language; medicine, science, and technology; and religion and philosophy. The collection also includes thousands of important works from the Americas.

The eighteenth century has been called "The Age of Enlightenment." It was a period of rapid advance in print culture and publishing, in world exploration, and in the rapid growth of science and technology – all of which had a profound impact on the political and cultural landscape. At the end of the century the American Revolution, French Revolution and Industrial Revolution, perhaps three of the most significant events in modern history, set in motion developments that eventually dominated world political, economic, and social life.

In a groundbreaking effort, Gale initiated a revolution of its own: digitization of epic proportions to preserve these invaluable works in the largest online archive of its kind. Contributions from major world libraries constitute over 175,000 original printed works. Scanned images of the actual pages, rather than transcriptions, recreate the works ***as they first appeared.***

Now for the first time, these high-quality digital scans of original works are available via print-on-demand, making them readily accessible to libraries, students, independent scholars, and readers of all ages.

For our initial release we have created seven robust collections to form one the world's most comprehensive catalogs of 18th century works.

Initial Gale ECCO Print Editions collections include:

> ### *History and Geography*
> Rich in titles on English life and social history, this collection spans the world as it was known to eighteenth-century historians and explorers. Titles include a wealth of travel accounts and diaries, histories of nations from throughout the world, and maps and charts of a world that was still being discovered. Students of the War of American Independence will find fascinating accounts from the British side of conflict.

Social Science
Delve into what it was like to live during the eighteenth century by reading the first-hand accounts of everyday people, including city dwellers and farmers, businessmen and bankers, artisans and merchants, artists and their patrons, politicians and their constituents. Original texts make the American, French, and Industrial revolutions vividly contemporary.

Medicine, Science and Technology
Medical theory and practice of the 1700s developed rapidly, as is evidenced by the extensive collection, which includes descriptions of diseases, their conditions, and treatments. Books on science and technology, agriculture, military technology, natural philosophy, even cookbooks, are all contained here.

Literature and Language
Western literary study flows out of eighteenth-century works by Alexander Pope, Daniel Defoe, Henry Fielding, Frances Burney, Denis Diderot, Johann Gottfried Herder, Johann Wolfgang von Goethe, and others. Experience the birth of the modern novel, or compare the development of language using dictionaries and grammar discourses.

Religion and Philosophy
The Age of Enlightenment profoundly enriched religious and philosophical understanding and continues to influence present-day thinking. Works collected here include masterpieces by David Hume, Immanuel Kant, and Jean-Jacques Rousseau, as well as religious sermons and moral debates on the issues of the day, such as the slave trade. The Age of Reason saw conflict between Protestantism and Catholicism transformed into one between faith and logic -- a debate that continues in the twenty-first century.

Law and Reference
This collection reveals the history of English common law and Empire law in a vastly changing world of British expansion. Dominating the legal field is the *Commentaries of the Law of England* by Sir William Blackstone, which first appeared in 1765. Reference works such as almanacs and catalogues continue to educate us by revealing the day-to-day workings of society.

Fine Arts
The eighteenth-century fascination with Greek and Roman antiquity followed the systematic excavation of the ruins at Pompeii and Herculaneum in southern Italy; and after 1750 a neoclassical style dominated all artistic fields. The titles here trace developments in mostly English-language works on painting, sculpture, architecture, music, theater, and other disciplines. Instructional works on musical instruments, catalogs of art objects, comic operas, and more are also included.

The BiblioLife Network

This project was made possible in part by the BiblioLife Network (BLN), a project aimed at addressing some of the huge challenges facing book preservationists around the world. The BLN includes libraries, library networks, archives, subject matter experts, online communities and library service providers. We believe every book ever published should be available as a high-quality print reproduction; printed on-demand anywhere in the world. This insures the ongoing accessibility of the content and helps generate sustainable revenue for the libraries and organizations that work to preserve these important materials.

The following book is in the "public domain" and represents an authentic reproduction of the text as printed by the original publisher. While we have attempted to accurately maintain the integrity of the original work, there are sometimes problems with the original work or the micro-film from which the books were digitized. This can result in minor errors in reproduction. Possible imperfections include missing and blurred pages, poor pictures, markings and other reproduction issues beyond our control. Because this work is culturally important, we have made it available as part of our commitment to protecting, preserving, and promoting the world's literature.

GUIDE TO FOLD-OUTS MAPS and OVERSIZED IMAGES

The book you are reading was digitized from microfilm captured over the past thirty to forty years. Years after the creation of the original microfilm, the book was converted to digital files and made available in an online database.

In an online database, page images do not need to conform to the size restrictions found in a printed book. When converting these images back into a printed bound book, the page sizes are standardized in ways that maintain the detail of the original. For large images, such as fold-out maps, the original page image is split into two or more pages

Guidelines used to determine how to split the page image follows:

- Some images are split vertically; large images require vertical and horizontal splits.
- For horizontal splits, the content is split left to right.
- For vertical splits, the content is split from top to bottom.
- For both vertical and horizontal splits, the image is processed from top left to bottom right.

Mrs. Charlotte Charke

A NARRATIVE of the LIFE OF *Mrs.* CHARLOTTE CHARKE,

(*Youngest Daughter of* COLLEY CIBBER, *Esq*,)

CONTAINING,

I. An Account of her Birth, Education, and mad Pranks committed in her Youth.

II. Her coming on the Stage, Success there, and sundry Theatrical Anecdotes

III. Her Marriage to Mr *Charke*, and its Consequences.

IV. Her Adventures in Mens Cloaths, and being belov'd by a Lady of great Fortune, who intended to marry her

V. Her being Gentleman to a certain Peer

VI. Her commencing Strolling - Player, with various and surprizing Vicissitudes of Fortune, during nine Years Peregrination

VII. Her turning Pastry Cook, &c in *Wales* With several extremely humourous and interesting Occurrences

Written by HERSELF.

This Tragic Story, *or this* Comic Jest,
May make you laugh, *or cry*——*As you like best*
Prologue *to* The What d'ye Call It.

LONDON

Printed for *W. Reeve*, in *Fleet Street*, *A Dodd*, in the *Strand*, and *E Cook*, at the *Royal-Exchange*

M DCC LV.

THE AUTHOR TO HERSELF.

MADAM,

THO' Flattery is universally known to be the Spring from which Dedications frequently flow, I hope I shall escape that Odium so justly thrown on poetical Petitioners, notwithstanding my Attempt to illustrate those WONDERFUL QUALIFICATIONS by which you have so EMINENTLY DISTINGUISH'D YOURSELF, and gives you a just Claim to the Title of a NONPAREIL OF THE AGE.

That thoughtless Ease (so peculiar to yourself) with which you have run thro' many strange and unaccountable Vicissitudes of Fortune, is an undeniable Proof of the native indolent

DEDICATION.

indolent Sweetness of your Temper. With what Fortitude of Mind have you vanquish'd Sorrow, with the fond Imagination and promissary Hopes (ONLY FROM YOURSELF) of a Succession of Happiness, neither WITHIN YOUR POWER OR VIEW?

Your exquisite Taste in Building must not be omitted The magnificent airy Castles, for which you daily drew out Plans without Foundation, must, could they have been distinguishable to Sight, long

vi DEDICATION.

ere this have darken'd all the lower World; nor can you be match'd, in Oddity of Fame, by any but that celebrated Knight-Errant of the Moon, G———E A————R S r———— s; whose Memoirs, and yours conjoin'd, would make *great Figures in History*, and might justly claim a Right to be transmitted to Posterity; as you are, without Exception, two of *the greatest Curiosities* that ever were the Incentives to the most *profound Astonishment*.

My

DEDICATION.

My Choice of you, Madam, to patronize my Works, is an evidential Proof that I am not disinterested in that Point; as the World will easily be convinc'd, from your natural Partiality to all I have hitherto produc'd, that you will tenderly overlook *their Errors*, and, to the utmost of your Power, endeavour *to magnify their Merits*. If, by your Approbation, the World may be perswaded into a tolerable Opinion of my Labours, I shall, for the Novelty-sake,

viii DEDICATION.

venture for once to call you, FRIEND; a Name, I own, I never *as yet have known you by*.

I hope, dear Madam, as MANLY says in *The Provok'd Husband*, that " LAST RE-" PROACH HAS STRUCK " YOU", and that you and I may ripen our Acquaintance into a perfect Knowledge of each other, that may establish a lasting and social Friendship between us.

Your

DEDICATION.

Your two Friends, PRUDENCE and REFLECTION, I am inform'd, have lately ventur'd to pay you a Visit; for which I heartily congratulate you, as nothing can possibly be more joyous to the Heart than the Return of absent Friends, after a long and painful Peregrination.

Permit me, Madam, to subscribe myself for the future,

x DEDICATION.

ture, what I ought to have been some Years ago,

Your real Friend,

And humble Servant,

Charlotte Charke.

A

NARRATIVE of the LIFE

OF

Mrs. *Charlotte Charke.*

AS the following History is the Product of a Female Pen, I tremble for the terrible Hazard it must run in venturing into the World, as it may very possibly suffer, in many Opinions, without perusing it; I therefore humbly move for its having the common Chance of a Criminal, at least to be properly examin'd, before it is condemn'd. And should it be found guilty of Nonsense

and

and Inconsistencies, I must consequently resign it to its deserved Punishment, instead of being honour'd with the last Row of a Library, undergo the Indignancy of preserving the Syrup of many a choice Tart, which, when purchas'd, even the hasty Child will soon give an Instance of its Contempt of my Muse, by committing to the Flames, or perhaps cast it to the Ground, to be trampled to Death by some Thread-bare Poet, whose Works might possibly have undergone the same Malevolence of Fate.

However, I must beg Leave to inform those Ladies and Gentlemen, whose Tenderness and Compassion may excite 'em to make this little Brat of my Brain the Companion of an idle Hour, that I have paid all due Regard to Decency wherever I have introduc'd the Passion of Love, and have only suffer'd it to take its Course in its proper and necessary Time, without fulsomely inflaming the Minds of my young Readers, or shamefully offending those of riper Years, a Fault I have often condemn'd, when I was myself but a Girl, in some Female Poets. I shall not descant on their Imprudence, only wish that their Works had been less confined to that Theme, which too often led 'em into Errors, Reason and Modesty equally forbid

In

In Regard to the various Subjects of my Story, I have, I think, taken Care to make 'em so interesting, that every Person who reads my Volume may bear a Part in some Circumstance or other in the Perusal, as there is nothing inserted but what may daily happen to every Mortal breathing.

Not that I would have the Publick conceive, tho' I am endeavouring to recommend it to their Protection, that my Vanity can so far overcome my small Share of Reason, as to impute the Success it should meet with to any other Motive, than a kind Condescension in my Readers to pity and encourage one, who has used her utmost Endeavours to entertain 'em.

As I have promis'd to give some Account of my UNACCOUNTABLE LIFE, I shall no longer detain my Readers in respect to my Book, but satisfy a Curiosity which has long subsisted in the Minds of many. And, I believe, they will own, when they know my History, if Oddity can plead any Right to Surprize and Astonishment, I may positively claim a Title to be shewn among the Wonders of Ages past, and those to come. Nor will I, to escape a Laugh, even at my own Expence,

pence, deprive my Readers of that pleasing Satisfaction, or conceal any Error, which I now rather sigh to reflect on, but formerly, thro' too much Vacancy of Thought, might be idle enough rather to justify than condemn

I shall now begin my Detail of the several Stages I have pass'd thro' since my Birth, which made me the last-born of Mr *Colley Cibber*, at a Time my Mother began to think, without this additional Blessing (meaning my sweet Self) she had fully answer'd the End of her Creation, being just Forty-five Years of Age when she produc'd her last, " THO' " NOT LEAST IN LOVE". Nor was I exempted from an equal Share in my Father's Heart; yet, partly thro' my own Indiscretion (and, I am too well convinc'd, from the cruel Censure of false and evil Tongues) since my Maturity, I lost that Blessing: Which, if strongest Compunction and uninterrupted Hours of Anguish, blended with Self-conviction and filial Love, can move his Heart to Pity and Forgiveness, I shall, with Pride and unutterable Transport, throw myself at his Feet, to implore the only Benefit I desire or expect, his BLESSING, and his PARDON.

But

But of that, more hereafter ---And I hope, ere this small Treatise is finish'd, to have it in my Power to inform my Readers, my painful Separation from my once tender Father will be more than amply repaid, by a happy Interview; as I am certain neither my present or future Conduct, shall ever give him Cause to blush at what I should esteem a justifiable and necessary Reconciliation, as 'tis the absolute Ordination of the Supreme that we should forgive, when the Offender becomes a sincere and hearty Penitent. And I positively declare, were I to expire this Instant, I have no self-interested Views, in Regard to worldly Matters; but confess myself a Miser in my Wishes so far, as having the transcendant Joy of knowing that I am restor'd to a Happiness, which not only will clear my Reputation to the World, in Regard to a former Want of Duty, but, at the same Time, give a convincing Proof that there are yet some Sparks of Tenderness remaining in my Father's Bosom, for his REPENTANT CHILD.

I confess, I believe I came not only an unexpected, but an unwelcome Guest into the Family, (exclusive of my Parents,) as my Mother had borne no Children for some few Years before, so that I was rather regarded as an impertinent Intruder, than one who had a natural Right to make up the circular Number of my Father's Fire-Side. Yet, be it as it may, the Jealousy of me, from her other Children, laid no Restraint on her Fondness for me, which my Father and she both testified in their tender Care of my Education. His paternal Love omitted nothing that could improve any natural Talents Heaven had been pleas'd to endow me with; the Mention of which, I hope, won't be imputed to me as a vain Self-conceit, of knowing more, or thinking better, than any other of my Sister Females. No! far be it from me, for as all Advantages from Nature are the favourable Gifts of the Power Divine, consequently no Praise can be arrogated to ourselves, for that which is not in ourselves POSSIBLE TO BESTOW.

I should not have made this Remark, but, as tis likely my Works may fall into the Hands of People of disproportion'd Understandings, I was willing to prevent an Error a weak Judgment might have run into, by inconsiderately throwing an Odium upon me, I could not possibly deserve----FOR, ALAS! ALL CANNOT JUDGE ALIKE.

As I have instanc'd, that my Education was not only a genteel, but in Fact a liberal one, and such indeed as might have been sufficient for a Son instead of a Daughter, I must beg Leave to add, that I was never made much acquainted with that necessary Utensil which forms the houswifely Part of a young Lady's Education, call'd a Needle, which I handle with the same clumsey Awkwardness a Monkey does a Kitten, and am equally capable of using the one, as Pug is of nursing the other.

This is not much to be wonder'd at, as my Education consisted chiefly in Studies of various Kinds, and gave me a different Turn of Mind than what I might have had, if my Time had been employ'd in ornamenting a Piece of Canvas with Beasts, Birds and the Alphabet, the latter of which I understood in *French*, rather before I was able to speak *English*.

As I have promis'd to conceal nothing that might raise a Laugh, I shall begin with a small Specimen of my former Madness, when I was but four Years of Age. Having, even then, a passionate Fondness for a Perriwig, I crawl'd out of Bed one Summer's Morning at *Twickenham*, where my

Father had Part of a House and Gardens for the Season, and, taking it into my small Pate, that by Dint of a Wig and a Waistcoat, I should be the perfect Representative of my Sire, I crept softly into the Servants-Hall, where I had the Night before espied all Things in Order, to perpetrate the happy Design I had framed for the next Morning's Expedition. Accordingly I paddled down Stairs, taking with me my Shoes, Stockings, and little Dimity Coat, which I artfully contrived to pin up, as well as I could, to supply the Want of a Pair of Breeches. By the Help of a long Broom, I took down a Waistcoat of my Brother's, and an enormous bushy Tie-wig of my Father's, which entirely enclos'd my Head and Body, with the Knots of the Ties thumping my little Heels as I march'd along, with slow and solemn Pace. The Covert of Hair in which I was conceal'd, with the Weight of a monstrous Belt and large Silver-hilted Sword, that I could scarce drag along, was a vast Impediment in my Procession: And, what still added to the other Inconveniencies I labour'd under, was whelming myself under one of my Father's large Beaver-hats, laden with Lace, as thick and broad as a Brickbat.

Being

Being thus accoutred, I began to consider that 'twould be impossible for me to pass for Mr. *Cibber* in Girl's Shoes, therefore took an Opportunity to slip out of Doors after the Gardener, who went to his Work, and roll'd myself into a dry Ditch, which was as deep as I was high; and, in this Grotesque Pigmy-State, walk'd up and down the Ditch bowing to all who came by me. But, behold, the Oddity of my Appearance soon assembled a Croud about me, which yielded me no small Joy, as I conceiv'd their Risibility on this Occasion to be Marks of Approbation, and walk'd myself into a Fever, in the happy Thought of being taken for the 'Squire.

When the Family arose, 'till which Time I had employ'd myself in this regular March in my Ditch, I was the first Thing enquir'd after, and miss'd; 'till Mrs. *Heron*, the Mother of the late celebrated Actress of that Name, happily espied me, and directly call'd forth the whole Family to be Witness of my State and Dignity.

The Drollery of my Figure render'd it impossible, assisted by the Fondness of both Father and Mother, to be angry with me; but, alas! I was borne off on the Footman's Shoulders,

Shoulders, to my Shame and Disgrace, and forc'd into my proper Habiliments.

The Summer following our Family resided at *Hampton-Town*, near the Court. My Mother being indispos'd, at her first coming there, drank every Morning and Night Asses Milk I observed one of those little health-restoring Animals was attended by its Foal, which was about the Height of a sizeable Greyhound

I immediately form'd a Resolution of following the Fashion of taking the Air early next Morning, and fix'd upon this young Ass for a Pad-nag, and, in order to bring this Matter to bear, I communicated my Design to a small Troop of young Gentlemen and Ladies, whose low Births and adverse States render'd it entirely convenient for them to come into any Scheme, Miss *Charlotte Cibber* could possibly propose. Accordingly my Mother's Bridle and Saddle were secretly procur'd, but the riper Judgments of some of my Followers soon convinc'd me of the unnecessary Trouble of carrying the Saddle, as the little destin'd Beast was too small, and indeed too weak, to bear the Burden, upon which 'twas concluded to take the Bridle only, and away went Miss and her Attendants,

who

who soon arrived at the happy Field where the poor harmless Creature was sucking. We soon seiz'd, and endeavour'd to bridle it, but, I remember, 'twas impossible to bring that Point to bear, the Head of the Fole being so very small, the Trappings fell off as fast as they strove to put them on One of the small Crew, who was wiser than the rest, propos'd their Garters being converted to that Use, which was soon effected, and I rode triumphantly into Town astride, with a numerous Retinue, whose Huzzas were drown'd by the dreadful Braying of the tender Dam, who pursued with agonizing Sounds of Sorrow, for her oppress'd young one.

Upon making this Grand-Entry into the Town, I remember my Father, from the violent Acclamations of Joy on so glorious an Occasion, was excited to enquire into the Meaning, of what he perhaps imagin'd to be an Insurrection, when, to his Amazement, he beheld his Daughter mounted as before described, preceded by a Lad, who scrap'd upon a Twelve-penny Fiddle of my own, to add to the Dignity and Grandeur of this extraordinary Enterprize.

I perfectly remember, young as I was then, the strong Mixture of Surprize, Pleasure, Pain

and

and Shame in his Countenance, on his viewing me seated on my infantical *Rosinante*; which, tho' I had not then Sense enough to distinguish, my Memory has since afforded me the Power to describe, and also to repeat his very Words, at his looking out of Window, *Gad demme! An Ass upon an Ass!*

But, alas! how momentary are sometimes the Transports of the most Happy? My Mother was not quite so passive in this Adventure, as in that before related; but rather was, as I thought, too active: For I was no sooner dismounted then I underwent the Discipline of Birch, was most shamefully taken Prisoner, in the Sight of my Attendants, and with a small Packthread my Leg was made the sad Companion with that of a large Table.

" *O! Fall of Honour!* "

'Tis not to be conceived, the violent Indignation and Contempt my Disgraise rais'd in my Infant-Breast, nor did I forgive my Mother, in my Heart, for six Months after, tho' I was oblig'd to ask Pardon in a few Moments of her, who, at that Time, I conceiv'd to be most in Fault.

Were

Were I to insert one quarter Part of the strange, mad Pranks I play'd, even in Infancy, I might venture to affirm, I could swell my Account of 'em to a Folio, and perhaps my whimsical Head may compile such a Work; but I own I should be loth, upon Reflection, to publish it, lest the Contagion should spread itself, and make other young Folks as ridiculous and mischievous as myself. Tho' I can't charge my Memory with suffering other People to feel the ill Effects of my unaccountable Vagaries; except once, I remember, a cross, old Woman at *Richmond* having beat me, I revenged myself, by getting some of my Playfellows to take as many as they could of her Caps, and other small Linnen that hung in the Garden to dry, and who sent 'em sailing down a Brook that forc'd its Current to the *Thames*, whilst I walk'd into the Parlour, secretly pleas'd with the Thoughts of my Revenge.

This is the only Piece of Malice that occurs to my Remembrance, but I have too much Reason to know, that the Madness of my Follies have generally very severely recoil'd upon myself, but in nothing so much as in the shocking and heart-wounding Grief for my Father's Displeasure, which I shall not impudently

impudently dare deny having justly incurr'd. But I dare confidently affirm, MUCH PAINS has been taken to AGGRAVATE MY FAULTS, and STRENGTHEN his Anger, and, in that Case, I am certain my Enemies have not always too strictly adher'd to TRUTH, but MEANLY had recourse to FALSHOOD to perpetrate the Ruin of a hapless Wretch, whose real Errors were sufficient, without the Addition of MALICIOUS SLANDERS. The Persons I mean, who did me these unfriendly Offices, are still in Being. But, *Qui Capit ille Facit.*

I formerly wrote to my Father, as I thought it an incumbent Duty to enquire after his Health, and, at the same Time, implore his Pardon, but could never have the Happiness of even a distant Hope of obtaining it. For the fore-mention'd Reasons I flatter myself, as Reflection and Contrition have brought me to a just Sense of all past Failings, HUMANITY will plead her Right in his RELENTING HEART, and once again restore me to a Joy which none can conceive, who never felt the Pain arising from the Disgrace of being deem'd an Alien from the Family, in which they originally drew Breath.

My

My Obligations to him in my bringing up are of so extensive a Nature, I can never sufficiently acknowledge 'em, for, notwithstanding 'tis every Parent's Duty to breed their Children with every Advantage their Fortunes will admit of, yet, in this Case, I must confess myself most transcendantly indebted, having received even a Superfluity of tender Regard of that Kind, and, at the same Time, beg Pardon for not having put it to a more grateful and generous Use, both for HIS HONOUR and MY OWN CREDIT.

However, I shall lay it down as a Maxim for the remaining Part of Life, to make the utmost Amends by PRUDENT CONDUCT, for the MISCARRIAGES OF THE FORMER; so that, should I fail in my Hopes, I may not draw any further Imputation on myself, by not endeavouring to deserve, what I think so particularly my Duty, if possible, to atchieve.

I shall now proceed in my Account. At eight Years of Age I was placed at a famous School in *Park-Street*, *Westminster*, governed by one Mrs *Draper*, a Woman of great Sense and Abilities, who employed a Gentleman, call'd Monsieur *Flahaut*, an excellent Master of Languages,

Languages, to instruct her Boarders. Among the Number of his Pupils, I had the Happiness of being one; and, as he discovered in me a tolerable Genius, and an earnest Desire of Improvement, he advised my Mother, in a Visit to me at School, to let him teach me *Latin* and *Italian*, which she, proud of hearing me capable of receiving, readily consented to.

Nor was my Tutor satisfied with those Branches of Learning alone, for he got Leave of my Parents to instruct me in Geography, which, by the Bye, tho' I know it to be a most useful and pleasing Science, I cannot think it was altogether necessary for a Female. But I was delighted at being thought a learned Person, therefore readily acquiesced with my Preceptor's Proposal.

Accordingly I was furnish'd with proper Books, and two Globes, cælestial and terrestrial, borrow'd of my Mother's own Brother, the late *John Shore*, Esq; Serjeant-Trumpet of *England*, and pored over 'em, 'till I had like to have been as mad as my Uncle, who has given a most demonstrative Proof of his being so for many Years, which I shall hereafter mention.

The

The vast Application to my Study almost distracted me, from a violent Desire I had to make myself perfect Mistress of it. Mr. *Flahaut*, perceiving that I was too close in the Pursuit of Knowledge not absolutely needful, shorten'd the various Tasks I had daily set me, thinking that one mad Mortal in a Family was rather too much, without farther Addition.

After I had received, in two Years schooling, a considerable Share of my Education (in which Musick and Singing bore their Parts) I was, thro' my indulgent Parents Fondness, allow'd Masters at Home to finish my Studies.

Mr. *Flahaut*, my Master of Languages, was continued. Mr *Young*, late Organist of St. *Clement's Danes*, instructed me in Musick, tho' I was originally taught by the famous Dr. *King*, who was so old, when I learnt of him, he was scarce able to give the most trifling Instructions. The celebrated Mr. *Grosconet* was my Dancing-Master, and, to do Justice to his Memory, I have never met with any that exceeded him in the easy sublime Taste in Dancing, which is the most reasonable Entertainment can be afforded to the Spectators, who wish only to be delighted

C with

with the genteel Movement of a Singular, or Plurality of Figures, with becoming Gracefulness, in which no Performer ever so eminently distinguished themselves as Mrs *Booth*, Widow of the late incomparable and deservedly-esteemed *Barton Booth*, Esq, one of the Patentees of *Drury-Lane* Theatre, conjunctive with my Father and Mr. *Wilks*.

The present Taste in Dancing is so opposite to the former, that I conceive the high-flown *Caprioles*, which distinguish the first Performers, to be the Result of violent Strength, and unaccountable Flights of Spirits, that rather convey an Idea of so many Horses *a la Manâge*, than any Design form'd to please an Audience with the more modest and graceful Deportment, with which Mrs. *Booth* attracted and charmed the Hearts of every Gazer.

When 'twas judged that I had made a necessary Progression in my Learning and other Accomplishments, I went to *Hillingdon*, within one Mile of *Uxbridge*, where my Mother, who was afflicted with the Asthma, chose to retire for the Preservation of her Health

This was an agreeable Retreat my Father had taken a Lease of for some Years, but a Winter Residence in the Country was not altogether

together so pleasing to me as that of the Summer, I therefore began to frame different Schemes, for rendering my Scheme as agreeable to myself as possible. The first Project I had, was in the frosty Mornings to set out upon the Common, and divert myself with Shooting, and grew so great a Proficient in that notable Exercise, that I was like the Person described in *The Recruiting Officer*, capable of destroying all the Venison and Wild Fowl about the Country.

In this Manner I employed several Days from Morn to Eve, and seldom failed of coming Home laden with feather'd Spoil, which raised my Conceit to such a Pitch, I really imagined myself equal to the best Fowler or Marksman in the Universe.

At length, unfortunately for me, one of my Mother's strait-lac'd, old-fashion'd Neighbours paying her a Visit, persuaded her to put a Stop to this Proceeding, as she really thought it inconsistent with the Character of a young Gentlewoman to follow such Diversions, which my Youth, had I been a Male, she thought would scarce render me excusable for, being but Fourteen. Upon this sober Lady's Hint, I was deprived of my Gun; and, with a half-broken Heart on the Occasion, resolved to revenge myself, by getting a Muscatoon that hung over the Kitchen Mantlepiece, and use my utmost Endeavours towards shooting down her Chimnies. After having wasted a considerable Quantity of Powder and Shot to no Purpose, I was obliged to desist, and give up what I had, though wishfully, vainly attempted.

I remember upon my having a Fit of Illness, my Mother, who was apprehensive of my Death, and consequently, thro' excessive Fondness, us'd all Means to prevent it that lay within her Power, sent me to *Thorly*, in *Hertfordshire*, the Seat of Dr. *Hales*, an eminent Physician and Relation, with a Design not only to restore and establish my Health, but with the Hopes of my being made a good Houswife; in which needful Accomplishment, I have before hinted, my Mind was entirely uncultivated. But, alas! she ENDED where, poor dear Soul, she ought to have BEGAN; for by that Time, from her Desire of making me too wise, I had imbibed such mistaken, pedantick Notions of a Superiority of Schollarship and Sense, that my utmost Wisdom centered in proclaiming myself a Fool! by a stupid Contempt of such Qualifications as would have rendered me less troublesome in a Family, and more useful to myself, and those about me.

Learning

Learning is undoubtedly a glorious and happy Acquisition, when it is encountered by a Genius capable of receiving and retaining the powerful Efficacy of its Worth, yet, notwithstanding this Assertion, I am certain that its greatest Advantages are to be infinitely improved by launching into the World, and becoming acquainted with the different Places and Objects we go thro' and meet in travelling.

The Observations to be made, by that Means, refine the Understanding and improve the Judgment, as something is to be gathered from the various Dispositions of People in the highest and lowest Stations of Life, which Persons of Reflection may render greatly conducive, in clearing and purging themselves of those Dregs of Learning which too often, for Want of this Method of purifying the Mind, reduces many a fine Genius to four Pedantry and ill Humour, that makes them uneasy to themselves, and obnoxious to all who converse with 'em.

Even in my slender Capacity, I have found this Remark to be just, for, notwithstanding my Vanity might have excited me to a fond Belief of my being wonderful wise, in nine Years Peregrination I began to find out, 'till I had seen something of the World, I was but rough in the Mine. Observation had a little polished me, and I was soon convinced the additional Helps I received from Travel, almost rendered my former Knowledge nothing: So that I cannot but join in *Polydore*'s Opinion;

" *I would be busy in the World, and learn;*
" *Not like a coarse and useless Dunghil*
    " *Weed,*
" *Fix'd to one Spot, and rot just as I grew*"

Though I must acknowledge, it is an equal Error for Youth to set out too soon to see the World, before they are capable of digesting what they hear or see, and too frequently come back with the same light Load of Understanding with which they set out; I therefore think it proper, instead of saying such a one is lately returned from his Travels (who is so unadvisedly sent forth) rather to have it said, *He is lately returned from his* DELIGHTFUL JAUNTS, AND PARTIES OF PLEASURE.

In the second Chapter of Mr. DUMONT's History I have expatiated on this Error, and refer my Readers thereto, who, I believe, will not think my Argument offensive or unreasonable.

While

While I staid at *Thorly*, though I had the niceſt Examples of houſwifely Perfections daily before me, I had no Notion of entertaining the leaſt Thought of thoſe neceſſary Offices, by which the young Ladies of the Family ſo eminently diſtinguiſhed themſelves, in ornamenting a well-diſpos'd, elegant Table, decently graced with the Toil of their Morning's Induſtry; nor could I bear to paſs a Train of melancholly Hours in poring over a Piece of Embroidery, or a well-wrought Chair, in which the young Females of the Family (excluſive of my mad-cap Self) were equally and induſtriouſly employed, and have often, with inward Contempt of 'em, pitied their Misfortunes, who were, I was well aſſured, incapable of currying a Horſe, or riding a Race with me.

Many and vain Attempts were uſed, to bring me into their Working-Community, but I had ſo great a Veneration for Cattle and Husbandry, 'twas impoſſible for 'em, either by Threats or tender Advice, to bring me into their SOBER SCHEME.

If any Thing was amiſs in the Stable, I was ſure to be the Firſt and Head of the Mob, but if all the Fine-Works in the Family had been

been in the Fire, I should not have forsook the Curry-comb, to have endeavoured to save 'em from the utmost Destruction.

During my Residence in the Family, I grew passionately fond of the Study of Physick; and was never so truly happy, as when the Doctor employed me in some little Offices in which he durst intrust me, without Prejudice to his Patients.

As I was indulged in having a little Horse of my own, I was frequently desired to call upon one or other of the neighbouring Invalids, to enquire how they did; which gave me a most pleasing Opportunity of fancying myself a Physician, and affected the Solemnity and Gravity which I had often observed in the good Doctor. Nor am I absolutely assured, from the significant Air which I assumed, whether some of the weaker Sort of People might not have been persuaded into as high an Opinion of my Skill as my Cousin's, whose Talents chiefly were adapted to the Study of Physick. To do him Justice, he was a very able Proficient, and, I dare say, the Loss of him in *Hertfordshire*, and some Part of *Essex*, is not a little regretted, as he was necessary to the Rich, and tenderly beneficent to the Poor.

At

At the Expiration of two Years his Lady died, and I was remanded Home, and once again sent to our Country-House at *Hillingdon*; where I was no sooner arrived, than I perfuaded my fond Mother to let me have a little Closet, built in an Apartment seldom used, by Way of Dispensatory. This I easily obtained, and summoned all the old Women in the Parish to repair to me, whenever they found themselves indisposed. I was indeed of the Opinion of *Leander* in *The Mock Doctor*, that a few physical hard Words would be necessary to establish my Reputation; and accordingly had recourse to a *Latin* Dictionary, and soon gathered up as many Fragments as served to confound their Senses, and bring 'em into a high Opinion of my Skill in the medicinal Science.

As my Advice and Remedies for all Disorders were designed as Acts of Charity, 'tis not to be imagined what a Concourse of both Sexes were my constant Attendants; though I own, I have been often obliged to refer myself to *Salmon*, *Culpepper*, and other Books I had for that Purpose, before I was able to make a proper Application, or indeed arrive at any Knowledge of their Maladies. But this Defect was not discovered by my Patients,

as

as I put on a Significancy of Countenance that rather served to convince them of my incomparable Skill and Abilities.

Fond as I was of this learned Office, I did not chuse to give up that of being Lady of the Horse, which delicate Employment took up some Part of my Time every Day; and I generally served myself in that Capacity, when I thought proper to pay my Attendance on the believing Mortals, who entrusted their Lives in my Hands. But Providence was extreamly kind in that Point, for though, perhaps, I did no actual Good, I never had the least Misfortune happen to any of the unthinking, credulous Souls who relied on me for the Restoration of their Healths, which was ten to one I had endangered as long as they lived.

When I had signified my Intention of becoming a young Lady *Bountiful*, I thought it highly necessary to furnish myself with Drugs, &c. to carry on this notable Design; accordingly I went to *Uxbridge*, where wa then living an Apothecary's Widow, whos Shop was an Emblem of that described in *Romeo and Juliet*. She, good Woman, know ing my Family, entrusted me with a Cargo o Combustibles, which were sufficient to hav set up a Mountebank for a Twelvemonth; bu my Stock was soon exhausted, for the silly Devils began to fancy themselves ill, because they knew they could have Physick for nothing, such as it was. But, Oh! woeful Day! the Widow sent in her Bill to my Father, who was intirely ignorant of the curious Expence I had put him to, which he directly paid, with a strict Order never to let Doctor *Charlotte* have any farther Credit, on Pain of losing the Money so by me contracted.

Was not this sufficient to murder the Fame of the ablest Physician in the Universe? However, I was resolved not to give up my Profession, and, as I was deprived of the Use of Drugs, I took it into my Head, to conceal my Disgrace, to have recourse to Herbs: But one Day a poor old Woman coming to me, with a violent Complaint of rheumatick Pains and a terrible Disorder in her Stomach, I was at a dreadful Loss what Remedies to apply, and dismissed her with an Assurance of sending her something to ease her, by an inward and outward Application, before she went to Bed.

It happened that Day proved very rainy, which put it into my strange Pate to gather up all the Snails in the Garden, of which, from the heavy Shower that had fallen, there was a superabundant Quantity I immediately
fell

fell to work; and, of some Part of 'em, with coarse brown Sugar, made a Syrup, to be taken a Spoonful once in two Hours. Boiling the rest to a Consistence, with some green Herbs and Mutton Fat, I made an Ointment; and, clapping conceited Labels upon the Phial and Gallipot, sent my Preparation, with a joyous Bottle of Hartshorn and *Sal Volatile* I purloined from my Mother, to add a Grace to my Prescriptions.

In about three Days Time the good Woman came hopping along, to return me Thanks for the extream Benefit she had received; intreating my Goodness to repeat the Medicines, as she had found such wonderful Effects from their Virtues.

But Fortune was not quite kind enough to afford me the Means of granting her Request at that Time; for the friendly Rain, which had enabled me to work this wonderful Cure, was succeeded by an extream Drought, and I thought it highly necessary to suspend any further Attempts to establish my great Reputation, 'till another watry Opportunity offered to furnish me with those Ingredients, whose sanative Qualities had been so useful to her Limbs and my Fame. I therefore dismissed her with a Word of Advice, not to tamper too much,

much, that as she was so well recovered, to wait 'till a Return of her Pains, otherwise a too frequent Use of the Remedy might possibly lose its Effect, by being applied without any absolute Necessity. With as significant an Air as I could assume, I bid her besure to keep herself warm, and DRINK NO MALT LIQUOR; and, that if she found any Alteration, to send to me.

Glad was I when the poor Creature was gone, as her harmless Credulity had rais'd such an invincible Fit of Laughter in me, I must have died on the Spot by the Suppression, had she staid a few Minutes longer

This Relation is an Instance of what I have often conceived to be the happy Motive for that Success, which Travelling-Physicians frequently meet with, as it is rather founded on the Faith of the Patient, than any real Merit in the Doctor or his Prescriptions But the Happiness I enjoyed, and still continue to do, in the pleasing Reflection of not having, through Inexperience, done any Harm by my Applications, I thank the Great Creator for, who (notwithstanding my extream Desire of being distinguished as an able Proficient) knew my Design was equally founded on a charitable Inclination, which, I conceive, was a strong

D   Guard

Guard againſt any Evils that might have accrued, from merely a wild Notion of pleaſing myſelf.

My being unfortunately deprived of the Aſſiſtance of the Widow's Shop to carry on this grand Affair, made me ſoon tire in the Purſuit, and put me upon ſome other Expedient for my Amuſement, I therefore framed the tendereſt Excuſes I could poſſibly invent to drop my Practice, that thoſe who had before thought themſelves indiſpenſibly obliged to me, might not conceive I had loſt that charitable Diſpoſition which they had ſo often bleſſed me for, and which, indeed, I heartily regretted the not having Power ſtill to preſerve and maintain.

My next Flight was Gardening, a very pleaſing and healthful Exerciſe, in which I paſt the moſt Part of my Time every Day. I thought it always proper to imitate the Actions of thoſe Perſons, whoſe Characters I choſe to repreſent, and, indeed, was as changeable as *Proteus*.

When I had blended the Groom and Gardener, I conceived, after having worked two or three Hours in the Morning, a broiled Raſher of Bacon upon a Luncheon of Bread in one Hand, and a Pruning-Knife in the other, (walking, instead of sitting to this elegant Meal) making Seeds and Plants the general Subject of my Discourse, was the true Characteristick of the Gardener; as, at other Times, a Halter and Horse-cloth brought into the House, and aukwardly thrown down on a Chair, were Emblems of my Stable-profession; with now and then a Shrug of the Shoulders and a Scratch of the Head, with a hasty Demand for Small-Beer, and a -----*God bless you make Haste, I have not a single Horse dressed or watered, and here 'tis almost Eight o'Clock, the poor Cattle will think I've forgot 'em, and Tomorrow they go a Journey, I'm sure I'd need take Care of 'em.* Perhaps this great Journey was an Afternoon's Jaunt to *Windsor,* within seven Miles of our House, however, it served me to give myself as many Airs, as if it had been a Progress of five hundred Miles.

It luckily happened for me that my Father was gone to *France,* and the Servant who was in the Capacity of Groom and Gardener, having the Misfortune one Afternoon to be violently inebriated, took it in his Head to abuse the rest of his Fellow-Servants, which my Mother hearing, interfered, and shared equally the Insolence of his opprobrious Tongue:

Tongue Upon which, at a Minute's Warning, he was difmiffed, to the inexpreffible Tranfport, my gentle Reader, of your humble Servant, having then the full Poffeffion of the Garden and Stables.

But what Imagination can paint the Extravagance of Joy I felt on this happy Acquifition! I was fo bewildered with the pleafing Ideas I had framed, in being actually a proper Succeffor to the depofed Fellow, I was entirely loft in a Forgetfulnefs of my real Self; and went each Day with that orderly Care to my feparate Employments, that is generally the recommendatory Virtue for the FIRST MONTH ONLY of a new-hired Servant.

The Rumour of the Man's Difmiffion was foon fpread, and reached, to my great Uneafinefs, to *Uxbridge*, and every little adjacent Village, upon which I foon found it neceffary to change my Poft of Gardener, and became, for very near a Week, Porter at the Gate, left fome lucky Mortal might have been introduced, and deprived me of the happy Situation I enjoyed.

I began to be tired with giving Denials, and, in order to put an End to their fruitlefs Expectations, gave out that we had received

Letters

Letters from *France*, to assure us, that my Papa had positively hired a Man at *Paris* to serve in that Office, and therefore all future Attempts would be needless on that Account.

I kept so strict a Watch at the Gate, during the Apprehensions I had of being turned out of my Places, the Maids wondered what made me so constantly traversing the Court-Yard, for near eight Days successively. But,

" *Alas! they knew but little of* Calista!"

'Twas really to secure my Seat of Empire; which, at that Time, I would not have exchanged for a Monarchy, and I conceived so high an Opinion of myself, I thought the Family greatly indebted to me for my Skill and Industry.

One Day, upon my Mother's paying me a Visit in the Garden, and approving something I had done there, I rested on my Spade, and, with a significant Wink and a Nod, ask'd, Whether she imagined any of the rest of her Children would have done as much at my Age? adding, very shrewdly, *Come, come, Madam, let me tell you, a Pound saved is a Pound got.* Then proceeded in my Office of Digging, in which I was at that Time most happily employed, and with double Labour pursued, to make the strongest Impression I could on my admiring Mother's Mind, and convince her of the Utility of so industrious a Child

I must not forget to inform the Reader, that my Mother had no extraordinary Opinion of the Fellow's Honesty whom she had turned away, and, what confirmed it, was tracing his Footsteps under the Chamber-Windows the Night after his Dismission, and the Neighbours had observed him to have been hovering round the House several Hours that very Evening

As we had a considerable Quantity of Plate, my Mother was a good deal alarmed with an Apprehension of the Man's attempting to break in at Midnight, which might render us not only liable to be robbed, but murdered. She communicated her Fears to me, who most heroically promised to protect her Life, at the utmost Hazard of my own Accordingly I desired all the Plate might be gathered up, and had it placed in a large Flasket by my Bedside This was no small Addition to my Happiness, as it gave me an Opportunity of raising my Reputation as a couragious Person, which

which I was extream fond of being deemed; and, in Order to establish that Character, I stripp'd the Hall and Kitchen of their Fire-Arms, which consisted of my own little Carbine (I had, through the old Maid's Persuasion, been barbarously divested of not long before) a heavy Blunderbuss, a Muscatoon, and two Brace of Pistols, all which I loaded with a Couple of Bullets each before I went to Bed, not with any Design, on my Word, to yield to my Repose, but absolutely kept awake three long and tedious Hours, which was from Twelve to Three, the Time I thought most likely for an Invasion.

But no such Thing happened, for not a Mortal approached, on which I thought myself undone; 'till a friendly Dog, who barked at the Moon, gave a happy Signal, and I bounc'd from my Repository with infinite Obligations to the Cur, and fir'd out of the Window Piece after Piece, re-charging as fast as possible, 'till I had consumed about a Pound of Powder, and a proportionable Quantity of Shot and Balls.

'Tis not to be supposed but the Family was, on my first Onset in this singular Battle (having nothing to combat but the Air) soon alarm'd. The frequent Reports and violent Explo-

Explosions encouraged my kind Prompter to this Farce, to change his lucky Bark into an absolute Howl, which strongly corroborated with all that had been thought or said, in Regard to an Attempt upon the House. My trembling Mother, who lay Half expiring with dreadful Imaginations, rang her Bell; which Summons I instantly obey'd, firmly assuring her, that all Danger was over, for that I heard the Villain decamp on the first Firing, which Decampment was neither more nor less than the Rustling of the Trees, occasioned by a windy Night, for the Fellow was absolutely gone to *London* the very Morning I declared War against him, as was afterwards proved.

Notwithstanding I was fully convinced I had nothing to conquer, but my unconquerable Fondness and Resolution to acquire the Character of a couragious Person, I settled that Point with the whole Family, in begging 'em not to be under the least Apprehension of Danger; urging, that my constant firing would be the Means of preventing any. And bid 'em consider, that the Loss of Sleep, was not to be put in Competition with the Hazard of their Lives.

This

This Reflection made them perfectly easy, and me entirely happy; as I had an unlimited Power, without Interruption, once in ten Minutes to waste my Ammunition to no Purpose And retiring to my Rest, as soon as my Stock was exhausted, enjoy'd in Dreams a second Idea of my glorious Exploits.

'Tis certain, nothing but my Mother's excessive Fondness could have blinded her Reason, to give in to my unprefidented, ridiculous Follies, as she was, in all other Points, a Woman of real good Sense. But where the Heart is PARTIALLY ENGAGED, we have frequent Instances of its clouding the Understanding, and MAKING DUPES OF THE WISEST.

I shall add one unfortunate Circumstance more, and then proceed to give an Account of my Marriage with Mr. *Richard Charke*; whose Memory will, by all Lovers of Musick who have heard his incomparable Performance on the Violin, be held in great Estimation. But to my Story ------ I had received Information, that there was a very fine young Horse to be disposed of at *Uxbridge*, qualified to draw a Chaise, and, having heard my
Father

Father say, before he went to *France*, he would purchase another when he came Home, I flew with distracted Joy to the Man's House, where this Horse was to be seen; and accordingly had him harnessed, and put to. This Excursion was entirely unknown to my Mother; who, at that Time, lay extreamly ill of the Asthma.

The Owner of the Horse, knowing my Family, and seeing me often drive my Father's Horses, made no Doubt but that I was sent in Fact to make Tryal of his; and, being willing to make his Market as quick as possible, got the Horse and Chaise ready in a few Minutes, and out I set, at the extream Hazard of my Neck, when I got upon *Uxbridge* Common : For the Creature was very young and ungovernable, and dragg'd me and the Chaise over Hills and Dales, with such Vehemence, I despaired of ever seeing *Hillingdon* again. However, the subtle Devil, knowing his Way Home, set up a barbarous full Gallop, and made to his Master's House with dreadful Expedition, beyond my Power to restrain ; and, in the Cart-rut, ran over a Child of three Years of Age, that lay sprawling there for its unfortunate Amusement.

The

The violent Rapidity of his Courfe luckily prevented the Death of the Child, but was very near effecting mine, for Grief and Surprize took fuch hold of my Spirits, I became fpeechlefs. The Child was foon brought after me by the Parents, attended by a numerous Mob, and, as foon as I regained my Speech, I order'd the Infant to be examined by a Surgeon But no Harm being done, more than a fmall Graze on the Neck, the Affair was made up with a Shilling and a Shoulder of Mutton

Notwithftanding this happy Acquittance from fo terrible a Difafter (as ignorant People are naturally fond of ftriking Terror) fome doubly-induftrious Courier, who had more Expedition than Brains, ran with the News to my Mother of my having kill'd a Child, which threw her into fuch agonizing Frights, as greatly hazarded her Life, and, for fome Time, was an Aggravation to the Illnefs fhe laboured under For though I came Home as foon as poffible, and convinced her of the Error of the ftupified Wretch that had fo cruelly alarmed her, the Surprize and Shock fo ftrongly poffeffed her, 'twas with Difficulty fhe retained her Senfes.

This

This Misfortune threw me into a Kind of Melancholly, that subsisted as long as could be expected from one of my Youth and volatile Spirits; and, to the extream Surprize of the Neighbourhood, Miss *Charlotte* became for a little while, I believe, rather stupidly dull, than justly reflecting. For I don't remember any Impression left on my Mind by this Accident after my Mother's Recovery, and the Assurance I had of the Boy's being living and well. However, it put a Period to the Fertility of my mischievous Genius, and, upon being soon after acquainted with Mr *Charke*, who was pleased to say soft Things, and flatter me into a Belief of his being an humble Admirer, I, as foolish young Girls are apt to be too credulous, believed his Passion the Result of real Love, which indeed was only Interest His Affairs being in a very desperate Condition, he thought it no bad Scheme to endeavour at being Mr *Cibber*'s Son-in-Law, who was at that Time a Patentee in *Drury-Lane* Theatre, and I in the happy Possession of my Father's Heart, which, had I known the real Value of, I should never have bestowed a Moment's Thought in the obtaining Mr. *Charke*'s, but preserving my Father's.

Alas!

Alas! I thought it a fine Thing to be married, and indulged myself in a passionate Fondness for my Lover, which my Father perceiving, out of pure Pity, tenderly consented to a conjugal Union. And the Reader may suppose that I thought, at that Time, 'twas the greatest Favour he ever conferred on me, as indeed I really did; but I have some modest Reasons to believe, had he indulged me under the Guardianship of some sensible trusty Person to have taken a small Tour into the Country, without letting me know 'twas done with a Design to break off my Attachment to my then intended Husband, it would have prevented the Match, and both Parties, in the Main, might have been better pleased; for I am certain that Absence, and an easy Life, would soon have got the better of the Violence of my Fondness, being then of too indolent a Disposition to let any Thing long disturb my Mind.

I don't advance this as a Reproach for my Father's Indulgence, but to give the Reader a perfect Idea of the Oddity of my youthful Disposition, for, as Sir *Charles Easy* says to his Lady, *He is often rude and civil without Design.* The same Inadvertency had an equal Dominion over me, and I have avoided or committed Errors, without any Premeditation either to offend or oblige.

But to my Tale ----- After six Months Acquaintance I was, by Consent, espoused at St *Martin*'s Church to Mr. *Charke*, and thought at that Time the Measure of my Happiness was full, and of an ever-during Nature. But, alas! I soon found myself deceived in that fond Conceit, for we were both so young and indiscreet, we ought rather to have been sent to School than to Church, in Regard to any Qualifications on either Side, towards rendering the Marriage-State comfortable to one another. To be sure, I thought it gave me an Air of more Consequence to be call'd Mrs. *Charke*, than Miss *Charlotte*, and my Spouse, on his Part, I believe, thought it a fine Feather in his Cap, to be Mr. *Cibber*'s Son-in-Law. Which indeed it would have proved, had he been skilful enough to have managed his Cards rightly, as my Father was greatly inclined to be his Friend, and endeavoured to promote his Interest extreamly amongst People of Quality and Fashion. His Merit, as a Proficient in Musick, I believe is incontestible, and, being tolerably agreeable in his Person, both concurr'd to render him the general Admiration of those Sort of Ladies, who, regardless of their Reputations,

make

make 'em the unhappy Sacrifices to every pleasing Object. Which, *entre nous*, was a most horrible Bar in my Eschutcheon of Content, insomuch, that married Miss was, the first Twelvemonth of her connubial State, industriously employed in the Pursuit of fresh Sorrow, by tracing her Spouse from Morn to Eve through the Hundreds of *Drury*.

I had, indeed, too often very shocking Confirmations of my Suspicions, which made me at last grow quite indifferent; nor can I avoid confessing, that Indifference was strongly attended with Contempt. I was in Hopes that my being blest with a Child would, in some Degree, have surmounted that unconquerable Fondness for Variety, but 'twas all one; and, I firmly believe, nothing but the Age of *Methusclah*, could have made the least Alteration in his Disposition.

This loose and unkind Behaviour, consequently made me extravagant and wild in my Imagination; and, finding that we were in the same Circumstances, in Regard to each other, that Mr *Sullen* and his Wife were, we agreed to part. Accordingly I made our Infant my Care, nor did the Father's Neglect render me careless of my Child, for I really was so fond of it, I thought myself more

than

than amply made Amends for his Follies, in the Possession of her.

When Mr. *Charke* thought proper he paid us a Visit, and I received him with the same good Nature and Civility I might an old, decay'd Acquaintance, that I was certain came to ask me a Favour, which was often the Case, for I seldom had the Honour of his Company but when Cash run low, and I as constantly supplied his Wants, and have got from my Father many an auxiliary Guinea, I am certain, to purchase myself a new Pair of Horns.

When I married 'twas in the Month of *February*, the Beginning of Benefit-time at both Theatres. Mrs. *Thurmond*'s coming on soon, who understood that I was designed for the Stage the Season following, requested that I might make my first Appearance on her Night, in the Character of *Mademoiselle*, in *The Provok'd Wife.* And, I particularly remember, the first Time of my playing, was the last in which that matchless Performer, Mrs *Oldfield*, ever charm'd the Town with her inimitable Exhibition. She sicken'd soon after, and linger'd 'till *October* following, when she expired, to the inexpressible Loss of her Acquaintance in general, and all Connoisseurs in Acting. Tho', I am apt to think, had she survived that Illness, the Stage would not have been less liable to have sustained her Loss, as she had acquir'd a considerable Fortune, and was in the Decline of Life, but, in her Business, still in the utmost Height of Perfection.

This excellent Actress, from her Encouragement, gave me lively Hopes of Success, and, being possessed with a youthful Transport, was rendered quite insensible of those Fears, which naturally attend People on their first Essay on the Theatre.

My Father and Mrs *Oldfield*'s Approbation, was no trifling Addition to my Self-conceit. 'Tis true, I was happy in a Genius for the Stage; but I have, since my riper Years, found that the Success I met with was rather owing to indulgent Audiences, that good-naturedly encouraged a young Creature, who, they thought, might one Day come to something, than any real Judgment I had in my Profession; and that I was more indebted to Chance than I was aware on, for the Applause I received, when I accidently stumbled on the Right.

I must beg Leave to give the Reader an Idea of that Extacy of Heart I felt, on seeing the Character I was to appear in the Bills; though my Joy was somewhat dash'd, when I came to see it inserted, *By a young Gentlewoman, who had never appear'd on any Stage before.* This melancholly Disappointment, drew me into an unavoidable Expence in Coach-hire, to inform all my Acquaintance, that I was the Person so set down in Mrs. *Thurmond*'s Benefit-Bills. Though my Father's prudent Concern intended it to be a Secret, 'till he had Proof of my Abilities.

To my inexpressible Joy, I succeeded in the Part, and the Play was in about six Weeks after re-chosen for the Benefit of Mr. *Charke* and Miss *Raftor*, now Mrs *Clive*, who was then a young, but promising Actress, of which she has given demonstrative Proofs, in various Lights, therefore shall not expatiate on that Subject, lest the Weakness of my Pen should fall short of her Merit.

My Name was in Capitals on this second Attempt; and I dare aver, that the Perusal of it, from one End of the Town to the other, for the first Week, was my most immediate and constant Business. Nor do I believe it cost me less,

less, in Shoes and Coaches, then two or three Guineas, to gratify the extravagant Delight I had, not only in reading the Bills, but sometimes hearing myself spoken of, which luckily was to my Advantage, nor can I answer for the strange Effect a contrary Report might have wrought, on a Mind so giddily loaded with conceited Transport------I'm not quite certain, whether my Folly and Indignation might not have caused a Drawn-Battle on such an Occasion.

It happened that Mrs. *Horton*, who played Lady *Fanciful* the Time before, was indisposed, and my Sister-in-Law, the late Mrs *Jane Cibber*, was appointed to do the Part, who, notwithstanding her having been a few Years on the Stage, and indeed a meritorious Actress, had not overcome the Shock of appearing the first Night in any Character. I, who was astonished at her Timidity, like a strange Gawky as I was, told her I was surprized at her being frighted, who had so often appeared; when I, who had never played but once, had no Concern at all. *That's the very Reason,* said she, *when you have stood as many Shocks as others have done, and are more acquainted with your Business, you'll possibly be more susceptible of Fear.* The Apprehensions she laboured under, gave her a

grave

grave Aspect, which my insensible Head at that Time took as an Affront, and, I remember, I turned short on my Heel, as we were waiting for our Cue of Entrance, and broke off our Conversation, nor could I bring myself, but on the Stage, to speak to her the whole Evening.

This ridiculous Circumstance we have both laughed at since, and I found her Words very true, for I'll maintain it, the best Players are the most capable of Fear, as they are naturally most exact in the Nicety of their Performance. Not that I would insinuate, by this Observation, that I think myself better than in the common Run of those theatrical Gentry, who are lucky enough to be endured through the Course of a Play, without being wished to be no more seen, after the First Act.

Such melancholly Instances I have been Witness of, both in Town and Country; WHILST THE POOR PLAYER HAS BAWLED AND BELLOWED OUT HIS MINUTE ON THE STAGE, AND THE GROANING AUDIENCE HISSINGLY ENTREATED, HE MIGHT BE HEARD NO MORE.

The second Character I appeared in was *Alicia*, and found the Audience not less indulgent

dulgent than before. Mrs *Porter*'s Misfortune, of being over-turned in her Chaise at *Highwood-Hill*, was the Means by which I was possessed of that Part. The third was the *Distress'd Mother*, in the Summer, when the young Company were under my Brother *Theophilus Cibber*'s Direction.

Now I leave to any reasonable Person, what I went through, in undertaking two such Characters, after two of the greatest Actresses in the Theatre, *viz.* Mrs *Oldfield* and Mrs. *Porter*. By this Time I began to FEEL I FEARED, and the Want of it was sufficiently paid home to me, in the Tremor of Spirits I suffered in such daring Attempts. However, Fortune was my Friend, and I escaped with Life, for I solemnly declare, that I expected to make an odd Figure in the Bills of Mortality------DIED ONE, OF CAPITAL CHARACTERS.

Soon after this *George Barnwell* made his Appearance on the Stage, in which I was the original *Lucy*, and, beginning to make Acting my Business as well as my Pleasure, the Success I had in that Part raised me from Twenty to Thirty Shillings *per* Week. After which, having the good Fortune to be selected from the rest of the Company as Stock-Reader to the Theatre, in Case of Disasters, I acquitted myself tolerably to the Satisfaction of the Masters and Audience.

My first Attempt of that Kind was *Cleopatra*, for the Benefit of Mr. *Worsdale*, who was honoured with the Presence of His Royal Highness the late Prince of *Wales*. Mrs *Heron* having that Afternoon the Misfortune to bruise her Knee-pan, she was immoveable; and I was, at the second Musick, sent for to read the Part.

Had I been under Sentence of Death, and St *Sepulchres* dreadful Bell tolling for my last Hour, I don't conceive I could have suffered much greater Agony; and thought of my Sister's Words to some Tune; for I absolutely had not a Joint or Nerve I could command, for the whole Night. And, as an Addition to the Terror I laboured under, Mr. *Quin*, THAT WORTHY VETERAN OF THE STAGE, played *Ventidius*. The Apprehension I laboured under in respect to the Audience, which was a numerous one, to the Amount of Three Hundred and odd Pounds, was nothing in Comparison to the Fright his Aspect threw me into.

But

But even this Shock I got through, and was soon after inducted to a second of the same Nature. Mrs *Butler* was taken ill, and the Queen in *Essex* was to be filled up: Accordingly, I was sent for to supply the Deficiency, which, in Justice to the Memory of the deceas'd Gentlewoman, I must inform the Reader she rewarded me for, by sending me, in a very polite Manner, a Couple of Guineas next Morning. I must needs say, I did not think it worth so handsome an Acknowledgement, but she sent in such a Manner that, had I refused it, I must have been guilty of a very great Absurdity, as her Station and mine at that Time were upon very different Footings, I being but a Babby in the Business, and she an established Person of a very good Salary.

I continued for that Season at the beforementioned Revenue, but, upon Mr *Highmore*'s making a Purchase in the Theatre, there immediately happened a Revolt of the greatest Number of the Company to the New Theatre in the *Hay-Market*. My Brother being principally concerned, I also made a Decampment, and was, by Agreement, raised from Thirty Shillings to Three Pounds, had a very good Share of Parts, and continued with them

them 'till the whole Body returned to Mr *Fleetwood*, who for some Time carried on the Business with great Industry, attended with proportionable Success; though, poor Gentleman, I fear that super-extraordinary Success was the Foundation of his Ruin.

It happened he and I had a Dispute about Parts, and our Controversy arose to such a Height, I, without the least Patience or Consideration, took a *French* Leave of him, and was idle enough to conceive I had done a very meritorious Thing. I cannot say, in the Affair, he used me entirely well, because he broke his Word with me; but I used myself much worse in the Main by leaving him, as I have since experienced. As there are too many busy Medlars in the World, who are ever ready to clinch the Nail of Sedition, when once 'tis struck; so some particular People thought it worth while, by villainous Falshoods, to blow the Spark of Fire between Mr. *Fleetwood* and myself into a barbarous Blaze, insomuch that I was provoked to write a Farce on the Occasion, entitled, *The Art of Management*; wherein the Reader may be assured I took no small Pains to set him in a most ridiculous Light, and spared not to utter some Truths which, I am sensible, ought rather to have been concealed. And

I cannot

I cannot but own, I have since felt some secret Compunction on that Score, as he, notwithstanding my impertinent and stupid Revenge, at my Father's Request, restored me to my former Station.

What further aggravates my Folly and Ingratitude, I made, even then, but a short Stay with him, and joined the late *Henry Fielding*, Esq, who, at that Time, was Manager at the *Hay-Market* Theatre, and running his Play, called, *Pasquin*, the eleventh Night of which I played the Part of Lord *Place*, which, 'till then, had been performed by Mr. *Richard Yates* But as he had other Parts in that Piece, Mr *Fielding* begged the Favour of him to spare that to make room for me, and I was accordingly engaged at Four Guineas *per* Week, with an Indulgence in Point of Charges at my Benefit, by which I cleared Sixty Guineas, and walked with my Purse in my Hand 'till my Stock was exhausted, lest I should forget the Necessity I then laboured under, of squandering what might have made many a decayed Family truly happy.

As I stand Self-convicted for all the Follies I have been guilty of, I hope my Behaviour to Mr *Flete-wood* will fix no Imputation, that may not be removed, and the less so, as I

might

might say to him from the Origin of our Quarrel, with *Peachum*,

" BROTHER, BROTHER, WE WERE
" BOTH IN THE WRONG "

My Motive for leaving him the second Time, proceeded from a Cause he had no Share in, which, I confess, is a farther Aggravation to my Ingratitude. I can only acknowledge my Error, and beg Pardon for the Folly, and, at the same Time, apologize for my Concealment of the Reason of my second Elopement, as 'twas partly a Family-Concern, though perhaps I might be condemned, were I to reveal it. But, notwithstanding I've done a Thousand unaccountable Things, I cannot absolutely think myself blameable for that last Project, farther than in using a Gentleman ill, who had behaved to me agreeable to that Character, when he might have taken any Advantages against me, without being thought guilty of Inhumanity or Injustice.

Soon after *Pasquin* began to droop, Mr *Lillo*, the Author of *George Barnwell*, brought Mr *Fielding* a Tragedy of Three Acts, called *The Fatal Curiosity*, taken from a true tragic Tale of a Family at *Penryn*, in *Cornwall*, who lived in the Reign of King
James

James the First. In this Play are two well-drawn Characters, under the Denominations of old *Wilmot* and his Wife *Agnes*, an aged Pair, who had, from too much Hospitality on the Husband's Part, and unbounded Pride on the Wife's, out-run a vast Estate, and were reduced to extreamest Poverty.

The late Mr *John Roberts*, a very judicious Speaker, discovered a Mastership in the Character of the Husband, and I appeared in that of the Wife. We were kindly received by the Audience, the Play had a fresh Run the Season following, and, if I can obtain a Grant for ONE NIGHT ONLY, I intend to make my Appearance once more as Mrs *Agnes*, for my own Benefit, at the *Hay Market* Theatre, on which Occasion, I humbly hope the Favour and Interest of my worthy Friends.

At the Time I was engaged with Mr *Fielding*, I lodged in *Overton-Street*, and boarded with my Sister *Brett*, who was but an Inmate as well as myself, but I, and my little Daughter, swelled up the Number of her Family. I being a Sort of Creature that was regarded as a favourite Cat or mischievous Monkey about House, was easily put off with what reasonable People might have deemed not only an Inconvenience, but an Affront; I accordingly was put into the worst Apartment, and was entirely insensible of it's Oddity, till a blustering Night roused me into an Observation of it's extraordinary Delicacy. When I had thoroughly surveyed it, I sat down and wrote the following Description of the Room, and exact Inventory of my Chattels.

Good People, for awhile give Ear,
Till I've describ'd my Furniture
With my stately Room I shall begin,
Which a Part of Noan's Ark has been
My Windows reach from Pole to Pole,
Strangely airy----that in Winter, o' my Soul,
With the dear Delight, of----here and there
 a Hole.

There is a Chest of Drawers too, I think,
Which seems a Trough, where Pigeons drink,
A Handkerchief and Cap's as much as they'll
 contain
O! but I keep no Gowns----so need not to com
 plain

Then, for my Fire, I've an Inch of Stove,
Which I often grieve I cannot move
When I travel from the Chimney t' th' Door,
Which are Miles full Three, if not Fourscore
         By

By that Time I, shiv'ring, arrive,
I doubtful grow if I'm alive.
Two foreign Screens I have, in Lieu
Of Tongs and Poker----nay, Faith, Shovel
    too.

Sometimes they serve to fan the Fire,
For 'tis seldom that to Bellows I aspire.
I'll challenge England's King, and the Pre-
    tender,
To say, that e'er I rust my Fender.

That Fashion's old, I've got a newer,
And prudently make use of Iron Skewer.
Now for my lovely Bed, of verdant Hue,
Which, ere Adam liv'd, might possibly be
    new

So charming thin, the Darns so neat,
With great Conveniency expel the Heat.
But these Things will not ever last,
Each Day a Curtain I, in breathing, waste.

Then, for Chairs, I indeed have one,
But, since Ruin draws so swiftly on,
Will lett my Room, ere Chair, Screens,
And Curtains all are gone.

These curious Lines were, for nineteen Years, preserved by my foolish, fond Sister, who, in her Turn, has been a universal Friend to her Brethren, or rather her Sisterhood. I wish Fortune had been less rigourous, and Gratitude more predominant; that the former might have prevented, or the latter have been the tender Motive to assuage those Sorrows and Inconveniencies of Life, she at present labours under. From which, as far as she has a Claim in me, and my poor Capacity extends, I'll make it the Business of my Life to extricate her, as I have, when Fortune was in her Power, been a Participater of her Bounty.

I don't make this Design publick with any Regard to myself, but with the pleasing Hope of being the happy Example to others, from whom she may have an equal Claim, both from NATURE AND GRATITUDE. Poor Thing! she is now in the five and fiftieth Year of her Age, and, as she has had no Faults the Family can alledge against her, 'tis Pity but she should be tenderly considered by 'em all, that the remaining Part of Life may pass away without those corroding Cares, that are too often the Impediment to our calling our Thoughts beyond the present State,

which,

which, alas! is the sad and dreadful Consequence of a FORGETFULNESS AND DISREGARD OF THE FUTURE.

I don't apprehend that to be my unhappy Sister's Case, for I'm certain her Reason and good Sense can never be reduced to such a Stupefaction, yet the strongest Intellects, and most resolute Minds, may possibly be vanquish'd in some Degree, by an oppressive Load of Anguish, and uninterrupted Hours of Care.

Now I am speaking of her, I must not omit the Mention of Mr *Joseph Marples*, her second Husband, the faithful Partner of her Sorrows, who is worthy the Consideration of every human Heart, as he tenderly endeavours to soften all her Distresses, which doubly preys on his Mind, from Want of Power totally to dissipate, and wears to her a pleasing Aspect, with a bleeding Heart. But I hope Providence has still an unforeseen Happiness in Store for 'em; and that I shall see their Clouds of Grief brighten'd with Smiles of Joy, from the Possession of a happier Fortune.

I must now leave them in the industrious and pleasing Search of what, I hope, they'll shortly obtain, and pursue my Story, by informing

forming my Reader, when I removed from my airy Mansion before-described, I took it into my Head to dive into TRADE. To that End, I took a Shop in *Long-Acre*, and turn'd Oil-woman and Grocer.

This new Whim proved very successful, for every Soul of my Acquaintance, of which I have a numerous Share, came in Turn to see my mercantile Face; which carried in it as conceited an Air of Trade as it had before in Physick, and I talk'd of myself and other DEALERS, as I was pleased to term it. The Rise and Fall of Sugars was my constant Topick, and Trading, Abroad and at Home, was as frequent in my Mouth as my Meals. To compleat the ridiculous Scene, I constantly took in the Papers to see how Matters went at *Bear-Key*; what Ships were come in, or lost, who, in our Trade, was broke, or who advertised Teas at the lowest Prices. Ending with a Comment upon those Dealers, who were endeavouring to under-sell us; shrewdly prognosticating their never being quiet, 'till they had rendered the Article of Tea a meer Drug, and THAT I, AND MANY MORE OF THE BUSINESS, should be obliged entirely to give it up. An Injury to Traffick in general! that must be allowed.

I must

I must beg Leave, gentle Reader, to tell you, that my Stock perhaps did not exceed ten or a dozen Pounds at a Time of each Sort, but that furnished me with as much Discourse, as if I had the whole Lading of a Ship in my Shop. Then, as to Oils, to be sure the famous *Nobbs*, and Fifty more, were not to be put in Competition with mine for their Excellence, and, though I seldom kept above a Gallon of a Sort in the House, I carried on the Farce so far as to write to Country Chapmen to deal with me.

Then I considered, 'till I had established a universal Trade, I'd save, for the first Year, the Expence of an Out-rider, as I was a very good Horsewoman, and go the Journies myself, concluding, with a significant Nod, that Money was as well in my own Pocket as another's ----But, providentially for me, I could gain no Country Customers, for, as the Case stood, I must positively have let 'em had the Goods considerably to my own Loss. And, as a Proof, will relate a Circumstance that occurred to me, in the selling a Quarter of a Hundred of Lump-Sugar to a good-natur'd Friend, who came to buy it for no other Reason, but that I sold it

'Tis

'Tis customary, in buying of Sugars by the Hundred, to be allowed a Tret of six Pounds *extra*. I was so insufferably proud of hearing so large a Quantity demanded by my Friend, that I really forgot the Character of Grocer, and, fancying myself the Sugar-Baker, allow'd in the twenty-five Pounds the Half of what I got in the Hundred; alledging, that 'twas our Way, when People dealt for large Quantities, to make an Allowance over and above the common Weight.

My Friend, who knew no better than myself, promised me all the Custom she could bring; which, if she had been as good as her Word, might in due Course of Time have paved the Way for me either to *Newgate*, the *Fleet*, or *Marshalsea*.

After my Friend was gone with her Bargain, I began (as I thought Trade encreasing) to think it proper to purchase a large Pair of Scales to weigh by Hundreds, and a large Beam to hang 'em on; and set out next Morning to that Purpose, traversing through *Drury-Lane*, *Holborn*, *Fleet-Ditch*, &c. but, meeting with nothing to my Mind, returned Home, with a Resolution to have a Pair made.

The

The good Woman who kept the House, upon hearing I had been endeavouring to make this needless Purchase, made bold to enquire into the Necessity of it: Upon which I told her, what had happened the Day before, and mentioned, as a Proof of my Knowledge of Trade, the Advantage I allowed to my Friend. She for some Time left me amazed at her Meaning, while she was almost strangled with laughing at my Folly.

When she came to herself, I gravely asked where the Joke lay, and what mighty Wonder there was in my having an encreasing Trade, who had such a universal Acquaintance? As soon as she was able to convince me of the Error I had committed, in giving one Half of the Over-weight in a Quarter of a Hundred, which was allowed in a whole Hundred only, I began to drop my Jaw, and looked as foolish as any reasonable Person may suppose, on so ridiculous an Occasion.

Links and Flambeaux are a Commodity belonging to the Oil-Trade, at least generally sold in Shops of that Kind, and constant and large Demands I had for both. But I remember, in particular, one of those nocturnal Illuminators, who are the necessary Conductors
for

for those who don't chuse Chairs or Coaches, came every Night just before Candle-time, which is the dusky Part of the Evening, the most convenient Light for perpetrating a wicked Intent, as will be proved in the Sequel of my Story.

To be sure I thought myself infinitely obliged to the sooty-colour'd Youth for using my Shop, and was mighty proud of his Handsel every Evening, and sometimes, as I dealt in spiritous Liquors, treated him with a Dram, and many Thanks for his own, and other Gentlemens Custom, of his Profession. The arch Villain smiled, and expressed great Satisfaction that even, in his poor Way, he had the Power of serving his good Mistress. He bow'd, and I curtsey'd; 'till, walking Backwards out of my Shop, he had complemented me out of every Brass Weight I had in it.

He had not been gone five Minutes, ere I had Occasion to make use of some of 'em, when, to my great Amazement and Confusion, not one was to be found. Unluckily for me, they were piled up one within the other, and injudiciously placed in the Corner of the Window next the Door, quite pat to his Purpose. And he was really so perfect a Master

of

of his Art in Filching, that, notwithstanding the great Ceremony that passed between us from the Upper-End of the Shop to the Lower, he went off entirely undiscovered in his Villainy.

I need not tell the Reader 'twas the last Interview we ever had, 'till I (to his great Misfortune) saw him making a small Tour in a two-wheel'd Coach from *Newgate* to *Tyburn*; a College where many an industrious 'Squire, like himself, have frequently and deservedly taken their Degrees.

This second *Fracas* so closely pursuing the former, I had some secret Thoughts of shutting up my Shop for ever, to conceal my Misfortunes and Disgrace, though I altered my Mind for that Time, but, I think, in about three Months after I positively threw it up, at a Hundred Pounds Stock, all paid for, to keep a grand Puppet-Show over the *Tennis-Court*, in *James-Street*, which is licenced, and which is the only one in this Kingdom that has had the good Fortune to obtain so advantageous a Grant.

When I first went into my Shop, I was horribly puzzled for the Means of securing my Effects from the Power of my Husband; who,

who, though he did not live with me, I knew had a Right to make bold with any Thing that was mine, as there was no formal Article of Separation between us. And I could not easily brook his taking any Thing from me to be profusely expended on his Mistress, who lived no farther from me than the House next to the Coach-Maker's, in *Great Queen's-Street*, and was Sister to the famous Mrs. *Sally K---g*, one of the Ladies of the HIGHEST IRREPUTABLE REPUTATION at that Time, in or about *Covent-Garden*. However, to prevent any Danger, I gave and took all Receipts ('till Mr *Charke* went to *Jamaica*, where he died in about twenty Months after his leaving *England*) in the Name of a Widow Gentlewoman, who boarded with me, and I sat quiet and snug with the pleasing Reflection of my Security, though he suspected I had a Hand in the Plot.

But he did not stay long enough to trouble me on that Score, for his Lady was one Day unfortunately arrested for a Hundred Pounds as they sat *Tête à Tête* at Dinner. And he, to show his Gallantry, went directly into the City and immediately purchased her Redemption, by taken up that Sum of the Merchants, who were Agents for the Gentleman he went over

over with, and whom, 'till then, he left in Uncertainty whether he would go or not.

It was concerted between this happy Pair, that Madam should follow, and, I suppose, pass in the *Indies* for his Wife, which she had my Leave to do, though she were a Lady.

As I have, among many other Censures, laboured under that of being a giddy, indiscreet Wife, I must take this Opportunity of referring myself to the superior Judgment of those who read my Story, whether a young Creature, who actually married for Love (at least I thought so, nay, was foolish enough to think myself equally beloved) must not naturally be incensed, when, in less than a Month after Marriage, I received the most demonstrative Proofs of Disregard, where I ought to have found the greatest Tenderness: To be even to my Face, apparently convinc'd of his infatiate Fondness for a Plurality of common Wretches, that were to be had for Half a Crown. This, consequently, raised in me both Aversion and Contempt, and, not having Years enough to afford me much Reflection, nor Patience sufficient to sit down like Lady *Easy*, contented with my Wrongs, 'till

Experience might by Chance have made him wiser.

Had he entertained a reciprocal Affection for me, he had, when I married him, so absolute a Possession of my Heart, 'twas in his Power to have moulded my Temper as he thought fit, but the ungrateful Returns my Fondness met with could not fail of the unhappy Effects, of a growing Disregard on my Side.

I was in Hope the Birth of my little Girl might have made some Impression on his Mind, but 'twas the same Thing after as before it; nor did he make the least Provision for either of us, when he went Abroad. 'Tis true, I was then in *Lincoln's-Inn-Fields* Playhouse, and from thence engaged at a good Salary with the late Mr *Fielding*; but then I was as liable to Death or Infirmities as any other Part of the Creation, which might have disempower'd me from getting my own, or my Child's bread.

Pray what was to become of us then? I laboured under the melancholly Circumstance, of being newly under my Father's Displeasure, and consequently no Redress to be hoped or expected from that Quarter, which he very well

well knew, and, as I have been since informed, was one of the principal Sowers of Sedition betwixt us. Though, at the same Time, he would explode my Father behind his Back, and condemn him to me, for the very Things he had partly urged him to.

However, though he did not chuse to be a HUSBAND or a FATHER, he proved himself a SON, by making an Assignment of Twenty Pounds a Year, during his Life, to his Mother, who constantly made it her Practice to be one of the Party with him and his Lady, and very confidently come from them to my Apartment, and give me a History of the Chat of the Day that had passed between them.

But Peace to his *Manes!* and, I hope Heaven has forgiven him, as I do from my Soul, and wish, for both our sakes, he had been Master of more Discretion, I had then possibly been possessed of more Prudence.

About a Year before he went to the *Indies*, I had the Misfortune to lose my dear Mother, otherwise I should not have undergone that Perturbation of Mind I suffered, from his not leaving any Thing, in Case of Accidents, for mine and the Child's Support, as my Mother's ther's Tenderness would have made us equally her Care, in any Exigence that might have occurred to me. But, alas! she was gone, to my Sorrow, even to the present Minute in which I mention her, and shall ever revere her Memory, as is quite incumbent on me, for her inexpressible Fondness and tender Regard for me, to the latest Moment of her Life.

This dear Woman was possessed of every personal Charm, that could render her attractive and amiable. Her Conquest over my Father, was by a Visit he made to her late Brother, whom I have before mentioned, and, as he passed by the Chamber, where she was accompanying her own Voice on the Harpsichord, his Ear was immediately charmed, on which he begged to be introduced, and, at first Sight, was captivated. Nor, as I hear, was she less delighted with the Sprightliness of his Wit, than he was with the Fund of Perfection with which Art and Nature had equally endowed her. In short, a private Courtship began, and ended in a Marriage against her Father's Consent, as Mr *Colley Cibber* was then rather too young for a Husband, in the old Gentleman's Opinion, he not coming to Age 'till after (as I have been told) the Birth of his second Child. But notwithstanding

withstanding my Grandfather, in the End, gave her a Fortune, and intended a larger, but this Marriage made him convert the intended additional Sum to another Use, and, in Revenge, built a Folly on the *Thames*, called *Shore's-Folly*, which was demolished some Years before I was born.

Her Father's Family, exclusive of her Children, is now entirely extinct, by the Death of my Uncle, who, poor Man, had the Misfortune to be ever touched in his Brain, and, as a convincing Proof, married his Maid, at an Age when he and she both had more Occasion for a Nurse than a Parson.

We have Proof positive of his being incapable of making a Will that can stand good, for which Reason I am determined, as being one of the Heirs at Law, to have a Trial of Skill with the ancient Lady, and see whether a proper Appeal to the Court of *Chancery* won't be the happy Means of setting aside a mad Man's Will, and make Way for those who have a more legal and justifiable Claim to his Effects, than an old Woman, whose utmost Merit consisted in being his Servant. I am only astonished they have let her alone so long, but I promise her she shall not find me quite so passive----and that right soon.

" And

"And HEAVEN give our Arms SUCCESS,
"As our CAUSE has JUSTICE IN IT."

For some Time I resided at the *Tennis-Court* with my Puppet-Show, which was allowed to be the most elegant that was ever exhibited. I was so very curious, that I bought Mezzotinto's of several eminent Persons, and had the Faces carved from them. Then, in regard to my Cloaths, I spared for no Cost to make them splendidly magnificent, and the Scenes were agreeable to the rest.

This Affair stood me in some Hundreds, and would have paid all Costs and Charges, if I had not, through excessive Fatigue in accomplishing it, acquired a violent Fever, which had like to have carried me off, and consequently gave a Damp to the Run I should otherwise have had, as I was one of the principal Exhibiters for those Gentry, whose Mouths were, like many others we have seen MOVE without any Reality of Utterance, or at least so unintelligible in the Attempt, they might as well have closed their Lips, without raising an Expectation they were unlucky enough to disappoint, whether ORATORS or PLAYERS, is not material. But as I have myself been lately admitted into the Number of the former, and from my Youth helped to fill up the CATALOGUE of the latter, I hope no Exceptions will be taken, as the Cap may as reasonably fit myself, as any other of either Profession, though I must beg Leave to hint, however deficient I, or some of my Cotemporaries may be, EVERY TRAGICK PLAYER, AT LEAST, SHOULD BE AN ORATOR.

'Tis no Complement to Mr *Garrick*, to say, HE IS BOTH, consequently Encomiums are needless to prove, what the nicest Judges have, for some few Years past, been so pleasingly convinced of.

'Tis, I own, natural and necessary to apologize for disgressing from a Subject, but, I hope, when the Reader considers the Merit of the Person who occasion'd it, I may, in the Eye of Reason and Judgment, stand excused. Perhaps, as Mr *Garrick* is a Person who many may undoubtedly wish to pay their Court to, this Remark may be deemed Adulation, but I must beg their Pardons, and assure them, they would, in that Point, be guilty of a very great Error, for I am the last Creature in the World to be picked out for that Piece of Folly. Nay, I think so meanly of it, as to set it down as Servility,

which

which I heartily contemn; and have been often blamed for a too Openness of Temper, that has sometimes hazarded the Loss of a Friend

In Regard to the above-mention'd Gentleman, there is not any Mortal breathing, that enjoys the Benefit of Hearing and of Sight, but must receive infinite Delight from his Performance, though they should be ever so indifferent to him, when off the Stage. But that is not my Case; I have received some Acts of Friendship from him, therefore of Course must revere him as a Benefactor, and am proud of this Opportunity to make him a publick Acknowledgement

'Tis certain, there never was known a more unfortunate Devil than I have been, but I have, in the Height of all my Sorrows, happily found a numerous Quantity of Friends, whose Commiseration shall be taken Notice of with the utmost Gratitude, before I close this Narrative. Now, ON TO THE AFFAIRS OF STATE.

When I quitted the *Tennis-Court*, I took a House, in *Marsham-Street*, *Westminster*, and lived very privately for a little while, 'till I began to consider, that my wooden Troop might

might as well be put in Action, and determined to march to *Tunbridge-Wells* at the Head of them. When I arrived, there was a General who had taken the Field before me, one *Lacon*, a famous Person, who had for many succeffive Years, and indeed, very succefsfully, entertained the Company with thofe inanimate Heroes and Heroines. I therefore was obliged to found a Retreat, and content myfelf with confining my Forces, and fighting againft *Lacon* in *Propria Perfona*, at *Afhley*'s Great Room.

I had living Numbers fufficient to play two or three of our thineft Comedies, and our only Tragedy we had to our Backs was *George Barnwell*, which I play'd for my own Benefit the laft Night, and fet out next Morning for *London*.

When I arrived there, I began to confider which Way I fhould turn myfelf. Being then out of the Houfes, and in no Likelihood of future Reftoration, I refolved to make the beft Ufe I could of my Figures, without fatiguing myfelf any farther, and lett my Comedians out for Hire to a Man, who was principally concerned in the Formation of them. But Bufinefs not anfwering his Ends and my Expectations, I fold, for twenty Guineas, what
coft

cost me near five hundred Pounds. Another Proof of my Discretion! and, indeed, of the Honesty of the Purchaser, that knew the original Expence of them, and the Reality of their Worth: But as I have condemn'd him for taking the Advantage of my Necessity, shall conceal his Name; and hope he'll have Modesty enough, if this Paragraph should be read to him, (by some who knew the Affair,) to add one Sin more, in denying that he was the Person.

I even gave him the Privilege, as I had a Licence, to make use of that and my Name, which now, when ever I think proper (as I shall never exhibit any Thing that can possibly give Offence) shall always employ Mr *Yeates*, who is a skilful Person, and one who has made it his Business from his Youth upwards.

As 'tis very possible I may entertain the Town with some unaccountable Oddity of that Kind very shortly, those that like to laugh I know will encourage me, and, I am certain, there is none in the World MORE FIT THAN MYSELF TO BE LAUGH'D AT. I confess myself an odd Mortal, and believe I need no Force of Argument, beyond what has been already said, to bring the whole Globe terrestrial into that Opinion.

It

It has been hinted (and indeed luckily came to my Ear,) that I should never have Patience to go through the Process of my Life. I don't suppose those who could advance such a Piece of Folly in me could possibly be my Friends, and am sorry for their Want of Humanity, as this Work is at present the Staff of my Life, and such an Insinuation must naturally deter many from taking it in, if they suppose me capable of such an Inconsistency. So far from it, that were I, by Miracle, capable of riding in my own Coach, I would still pursue my Scheme, 'till I had brought it to a Conclusion, for, a happy Change of Circumstances makes

"*Misfortunes past prove Stories of Delight,*"

And what now is my SUPPORT, would then be my AMUSEMENT.

'Tis strange! but true! let People use the most honest Endeavours to support themselves, there is generally some ridiculous Mortal that, without Rhime or Reason, and for the sake of saying something, without any real Views of Good or Ill, are often detrimental to the Industrious or Oppressed. Be it as it may, 'tis an Error, I fear, INVINCIBLE and HURT-

FUL TO BOTH, and sure, unprovoked to offer an Injury, IS UNPARDONABLE! If the contrary were the Case, 'tis NOBLER FAR TO OVER-LOOK THAN RESENT, but, as I have no Reason to believe that I have offended, I hope for the future no Person will be indiscreet enough to assert that for a TRUTH, which Time will prove to be a real FALSHOOD.

Not long after I had parted from what might really, by good Management, have brought me in a very comfortable Subsistance, and in a genteel Light, I was addressed by a worthy Gentleman (being then a Widow) and closely pursued 'till I consented to an honourable, though very secret Alliance; and, in Compliance to the Person, bound myself by all the Vows sincerest Friendship could inspire, never to confess who he was. Gratitude was my Motive to consent to this Conjunction, and extream Fondness was his Inducement to request it. To be short, he soon died, and, unhappily for me, not only from sustaining the Loss of a valuable and sincere Friend, but by the unexpected Stroke of Death, I was deprived of every Hope and Means of a Support.

As I have overcome all the Inconveniencies of Life this terrible Shock of Fate rendered me liable to, I am contented, and think myself happy; but not even the most inexplicable Sorrows I was immers'd in ever did, nor shall any Motive whatever make me break that Vow I made to the Person, by a Discovery of his Name.

This was a Means indeed, by which I hoped to have secured myself far above those Distresses I have known; but, alas! proved the FATAL CAUSE OF ALL. I was left involved with Debts I had no Means of paying; and, through the villainous Instigation of a wicked drunken Woman, was arrested for seven Pounds, when, as Heaven shall judge me, I did not know where to raise as many Pence.

The Officer who had me in Custody, on hearing my Story, really compassionated me, and was exceeding angry at the Woman, who, without Cause, worked up the Creditor to believe I had a Fortune of five Hundred *per Annum* left me, which was not in the Power of the Deceased to leave, nor as the Affair was a Secret, and Death sudden, any Probability of such a Happiness.

This Misfortune was occasioned first by the Stupidity and Cruelty of the Woman, and effected by Dint of a very handsome lac'd Hat I had on, being then, for some substantial Reasons, EN CAVALIER, which was so well described, the Bailiff had no great Trouble in finding me.

Undoubtedly I was extream happy, when he told me his Business! Having nothing in View but the *Marshalsea*, the Gates of which I thought, though at that Time in the Middle of *Covent-Garden*, stood wide open for my Reception. But as the Man had Humanity, he eased me of those Fears, and, by Dint of a trifling Favour, conferr'd by poor Mrs. *Elizabeth Careless*, (whose Name will, I believe, be for some Years in Remembrance) I was set at Large, 'till Matters could be accommodated.

'Tis not to be expressed, the Transport I felt on his leaving me behind him with Mrs *Careless*, and her good-natur'd Friend, who, being an Attorney, was incapable of becoming my Bail, but compassionated my Distress, and sent me directly to Mr *Myrton*, who kept the *Cross-Keys*, requesting him to do that friendly Office for me, and sent by me a

Note

Note of Indemnification, which Mr *Mytton* could on no Means make any Exceptions to, as the Gentleman was a Person of Worth and Honour, and besides, a particular good Customer to the other.

The next Thing was to procure another Bail, to join with the former. I soon obtained one, whose good Nature was easily excited to do a kind Action, but, when I went to the Officer and told who it was, Objections were made against him, as he was obliged himself to keep close, for fear of an equal Disaster, and, to convince me of his Danger, produced a Writ which had been two or three Times renewed, to no Purpose.

What to do in this terrible Exigence I could not tell, as I had but a Day and a Half longer to be at Large, if I could not produce a second Bail. I tried all Means, but in vain, and, on the *Friday* following, was obliged to surrender, and lay that Night in *Jackson's-Alley*, at the Officer's House.

I had not been there Half an Hour, before I was surrounded with all the Ladies who kept Coffee-Houses in and about the *Garden*, each offering Money for my Ransom. But nothing

thing then could be done, without the Debt and Costs, which, though there was, I believe, about a dozen or fourteen Ladies present, they were not able to raise. As far as their Finances extended, they made an Offer of 'em, and would have given Notes jointly or separately, for the Relief of poor Sir *Charles*, as they were pleased to stile me. 'Tis true, the Officer would willingly have come into their kind Propositions, as he was truly sensible of my Indigence, but, being closely watched by the Creditor, who would, on no Terms be brought to any Composition, all their Efforts were ineffectual.

After two or three Hours wasted in fruitless Entreaties, it growing late, they left me to bewail the terrible Scene of Horror that presented to my tortured View, and, with a Heart over-charged with Anguish, and hopeless of Redress, I retired to my Dormitory, and passed the Night in bitterest Reflections on my melancholly Situation.

My poor Child, who was then but eight Years of Age, and whose sole Support was on her HAPLESS, FRIENDLESS MOTHER, knew not what was become of me, or where to seek me, and, with watchful Care, wore away

away the tedious Night, in painful Apprehensions of what really had befallen me.

About Seven next Morning, I dispatched a Messenger to my poor little suffering Infant, who soon came to me, with her Eyes overflowed with Tears, and a Heart full of undissembled Anguish. She immediately threw her Head upon my Bosom, and remained in speechless Grief, with which I equally encountered her. For some Time the Child was so entirely sensible of our Misfortunes, and of the Want of Means of being extricated from them, 'twas with Difficulty I soothed her into a Calm. Alas! what has the POOR and FRIENDLESS TO HOPE FOR! surrounded with Sorrows of such a Nature, that even People in tolerable Circumstances find some Perplexity, when SO ASSAILED, to OVERCOME?

I sat down and wrote eight and thirty Letters before I stirred out of my Chair, some of which went where I thought NATURE might have put in HER CLAIM, but I could obtain no Answer, and, where I LEAST EXPECTED, I FOUND REDRESS!

My poor little Wench was the melancholly Messenger, and neither eat or drank 'till she had

had faithfully discharged the Trust I reposed in her. To be short, the very Ladies who had visited me the Night before, brought with them the late Mrs *Elizabeth Hughes*, who, by Dint of her laying down a Couple of Guineas, and a Collection from the rest, with a Guinea from Mrs. *Douglass* in the *Piazza*, I was set at Liberty, and the Officer advised me to change Hats with him, that being the very Mark by which I was unfortunately distinguished, and made known to him.

My Hat was ornamented with a beautiful Silver Lace, little the worse for wear, and of the Size which is now the present Taste, the Officer's a large one, cocked up in the Coachman's Stile, and weightened with a horrible Quantity of Crape, to secure him from the Winter's Cold.

As to my Figure, 'tis so well known it needs no Description; but my Friend, the Bailiff, was a very short, thick, red-faced Man: Of such a Corpulency, he might have appeared in the Character of *Falstaff*, without the artful Assistance of Stuffing, and his Head proportionable to his Body, consequently we each of us made very droll Figures; he with his little laced Hat, which appeared on

his

his Head of the Size of those made for the *Spanish* Ladies, and my unfortunate Face smothered under his, that I was almost as much incommoded as when I marched in the Ditch, under the insupportable Weight of my Father's

However, this smoaky Conveniency (for it stunk insufferably of Tobacco) was a Security and absolute Prevention from other threatning Dangers, and I prudently retired into a most dismal and solitary Mansion in *Great Queen's-Street*, where I was hourly apprehensive of having the House fall upon my Head, though if it had, according to the old Proverb, it would not have been the first Misfortune of the Kind that had befallen me. 'Twas the old Building, which has since been formed into several new and handsome Houses.

When my kind Redeemers took me away, they treated me with an elegant Supper, and sent me Home to my Child with a Guinea in my Pocket, which they very politely desired me to accept on, as a Present to her.

I passed the Night in grateful Thoughts, both to Heaven, and those appointed by that Great Power to save me from the Gulph of absolute Destruction. I never having been in
a Distress

a Distress of that kind before, laid my Sorrow deeper to Heart; and the inexpressible Delight of being restored to my Child and Liberty, was almost too much for my fluttered Spirits at that Time to bear. So unexpected a Relief may be deemed a Prodigy! But what is there so difficult or unlikely, in the Imagination of thoughtless Mortals, that the All-Gracious Ruler of the World cannot bring to bear?

This very Circumstance convinces me that no Misfortune, of ever so dreadful a Nature, should excite us to despair. What had I to conceive, but the miserable Enforcement to linger out a wretched Life in Prison? A Child, who might possibly have been despised only for being mine; and, perhaps, reduced to Beggary.

These were the entertaining Ideas I had the Night of my Confinement; but, when I found Providence had been so tenderly and industriously employed in my Behalf, I began to arraign myself for supposing that my Relations, in such Extremity, though they were regardless of me, would have abandoned an innocent and hapless Child to that rigourous Fate my Fears suggested

During my solitary Residence in *Queen's-Street*, I never made my Appearance, for a considerable Time, but on a *Sunday*, and was obliged to have recourse to as many Friends as I could muster up, to help me to a Support for myself and my little Fellow-Sufferer. She, poor Child! was so deeply affected with the Malevolence of my Fortune, it threw her into a very dangerous Illness, but, even in that Distress, Heaven raised a Friend. My Brother *Theophilus Cibber*, kindly sent an Apothecary, at his own Expence; for which I shall ever acknowledge myself extreamly his Debtor, and am sorry I have not the Power of making a more suitable Return.

I left the poor Girl one *Sunday*, to prog for her and myself, by pledging with an Acquaintance a beautiful Pair of Sleeve-Buttons, which I effected in about two Hours, and, on my Return, asking the Landlady how the Child did, having left her very much indisposed. She told me, Miss went up, about an Hour and Half ago, to put on some clean Linnen, but, by her staying, she concluded she was lain down, having complained of being very sleepy before she went up. But, Oh! Heaven! how vast was my Grief and

Surprize when I entered the Room, and found the poor little Soul stretched on the Floor, in strong Convulsion Fits, in which she had lain a considerable Time, and no Mortal near to give her the least Assistance.

I took her up, and, overcome with strong Grief, immediately dropped her on the Floor, which I wonder did not absolutely end her by the Force of the Fall, as she was in Fact a dead Weight. My screaming and her falling raised the House, and, in the Hurry of my Distraction, I run into the Street, with my Shirt-Sleeves dangling loose about my Hands, my Wig standing on End,

"*Like Quills upon the fretful Porcupine,*"

And proclaiming the sudden Death of my much-beloved Child, a Crowd soon gathered round me, and, in the Violence of my Distraction, instead of administring any necessary Help, wildly stood among the Mob to recount the dreadful Disaster.

The Peoples Compassion was moved, 'tis true, but, as I happened not to be known to them, it drew them into Astonishment, to see the Figure of a young Gentleman, so extravagantly grieved for the Loss of a Child. As I
appeared

appeared very young, they looked on it as an unprecedented Affection in a Youth, and began to deem me a Lunatick, rather then that there was any Reality in what I said.

One of the People who had been employed in the Care, as I then thought, of my expiring Infant, missing me, sought me out and brought me Home, where I found the Child still in violent Convulsions, which held her from *Sunday* Eleven o'Clock in the Forenoon, without Intermission, 'till between the Hours of Eight and Nine next Morning.

In the Midst of this Scene of Sorrow, Mr. *Adam Hallam*, who lived next Door to my Lodging, hearing of my Misfortune, in a very genteel and tender Manner, proved himself a REAL FRIEND, UNASKED. The first Instance I had of his Humanity, was a Letter of Condolence, in which was enclosed that necessary and never-failing Remedy for every Evil, incidental to Mankind in general. And what was more extraordinary, was his constantly sending to enquire after the Child's Health, with the same respectful Regard as might have been expected had I been possessed of that Affluence I but some few Months before enjoyed.

At his own Request, his Table was my own, and, I am certain, his good Nature laid an Embargo on his Person, as he often dined at Home in Compliment to me, rather than leave me to undergo the Shock of mingling with his Servants, or be distinguished by them as his Pensioner, by leaving me to eat by myself.

It happened, very *à propos* for me, that Mr *Hallam* had a Back-Door into his House, which prevented the Hazards I might otherwise have been liable to, by going into the Street. And indeed, as *Sharp* says to *Gayless*, THE BACK-DOOR I ALWAYS THOUGHT THE SAFEST, by which Means I had a frequent Opportunity of conversing with a sincere Friend, whose Humanity asswaged the Anguish of my Mind, and whose Bounty was compassionately employed, for a considerable Time, to protect me and mine from the insupportable and distracting Fears of Want.

After what I have said, in regard to the Favours I received, I am certain no Person who ever knew what it was to be obliged, and had Honesty enough to DARE TO BE GRATEFUL, will condemn me for making this publick Acknowledgement, who have no
other

other Means of doing Justice to one, that had no Motive or Right to give such an Instance of Benevolence, but excited alone from a natural Propensity to do a good Action.

Favours, when received, are too often forgot, and I have observed Gratitude to be a Principle, that bears the smallest Share in the Hearts of those where it ought to be most strongly President, so that I begin to imagine one Half of the World don't understand the real Etymology of the Word.

But that I may give farther Assurances of my Detestation of that SIN OF UNKINDNESS AND INSOLENCE, I shall proceed to give a farther Account of Obligations I received from Strangers, and shall begin with those conferred on me by the late Mr. *Delane*, Comedian, who, though almost a STRANGER TO MY PERSON, grew INTIMATE WITH MY AFFLICTION, and testified his Concern, by raising a timely Contribution to alleviate my Distress, and redoubled the favourable Remedy, in the Politeness of the Application.

Mrs *Woffington* stands equally in the Rank of those, whose Merits must be founded in the Song of grateful Praise, and many more of the generous Natives of *Ireland*, who are, in Nature, a Set of worthy People, when they meet with Objects of Pity. And I have made bold to expatiate, in a particular Manner, on that Subject in my History of Mr *Dumont*, which will be immediately published, after the Conclusion of this Narrative.

I must now mention the friendly Assistance of Mr *Rich*, Mr *Garrick*, Mr *Lacey* (the several Governors of the two Theatres) Mr. *Beard*, and many more of the Gentlemen of the Stage, to whose Bounty I shall ever think myself indebted.

I am now going to take Notice of a Person who, at FRIENDLY DISTANCE, has many Times afforded a happy Relief to my bitterest Wants, namely, the present Mrs *Cibber*, whose Pity was once the Means of saving my Life, by preventing my going to a Jail. And more than once or twice fed both myself and Child, by timely Presents, only from HEARING of the sad Circumstances we laboured under. Whatever the World may think, in regard to my taking this publick Notice of her Humanity, I must beg to be excused, if I insist on my being JUSTIFIABLE BY THE LAWS OF GRATITUDE; and, as I was GLAD TO BE OBLIGED, should think it the

Height

Height of Insolence, to be ASHAMED TO MAKE THE ACKNOWLEDGMENT.

As soon as my poor Girl began a little to recover, I sometimes used, by OWL-LIGHT, to creep out, in Search of Adventures, and, as there was frequently Plays acted at the *Tennis Court*, with trembling Limbs and aching Heart, adventured to see (as I was universally studied) whether there was any Character wanting; a Custom very frequent among the Gentry who exhibited at that celebrated Slaughter-House of Dramatick Poetry.

One Night, I remember, *The Recruiting Officer* was to be PERFORMED, as they were pleased to call it, for the Benefit of a young Creature who had never played before. To my unbounded Joy, Captain *Plume* was so very unfortunate, that he came at Five o'Clock to inform the young Gentlewoman he did not know a Line of his Part. I (who, though shut up in the *Mock Green-Room*) did not dare to tell them I could do it, for fear of being heard to speak, and that the Sound of my Voice, which is particular, and as well known as my Face, should betray me to those Assailants of Liberty, who constantly attended every Play-Night there, to the inexpressible Terror of many a Potentate, who has quiveringly

quiveringly tremored out the Hero, lest the
the Catastrophe should rather end in a Spung-
House, than a Bowl of Poison or a timely
Dagger----The want of which latter Instrument of Death, I once saw supplied with a
Lady's Busk, who had just Presence of Mind
sufficient to draw it from her Stays, and end
at once her wretched Life, *and more wretched
Acting*.

Some of these kind of meritorious Exhibiters were to Massacre poor *Farquhar* that
Night, but not one among them capable of
playing, or rather going on for *Plume*,
which they would have done perhaps, like a
Chair set up to fill up the Number in a
Country-Dance. At last the Question was
put to me. I immediately replied (seeing the
Coast clear) I could do such a Thing, but,
like *Mosca*, was resolved to stand on Terms,
and make a Merit of Necessity. *To be sure,
Ma'am*, says I, *I'd do any any Thing to
oblige you. But I'm quite unprepared-----I
have nothing here proper-----I want a Pair
of White Stockings, and clean Shirt---*
Though, between Friends, in Case of a lucky
Hit, I had all those Things ready in my Coat-
Pocket, as I was certain, let what Part would
befal me, Cleanliness was a necessary Ingredient.

Then

Then I urged, That 'twould be scarce worth her while to pay me my Price. Upon which she was immediately jogged by the Elbow, and took aside to advise her to offer me a Crown. I, being pretty well used to the little Arts of those worthy Wights, received the Proposal soon after, and, without making any Answer to it, jogged the Lady's *other Elbow, and withdrew*, assuring her, that under a Guinea I positively would not undertake it. That, to prevent any Demur with the rest of the People, she should give me the Sixteen Shillings privately, and publickly pay me Five.

Her House was as full as it could hold, and the Audience clattering for a Beginning. At length she was obliged to comply with my Demands, and I got ready with utmost Expedition. When the Play (which was, in Fact, A FARCE TO ME) was ended, I thought it mighty proper to stay 'till the Coast was clear, that I might carry off myself and Guinea securely. But, in order to effect it, I changed Cloaths with a Person of low Degree, whose happy Rags, and the kind Covert of Night, secured me from the Dangers I might have otherwise encountered. My Friend took one Road I another, but met at my Lodgings,

ings, where I rewarded him, poor as I was, with a Shilling, which, at that Time, I thought a competent Fortune for a younger Child.

It happened, not long after, that I was applied to by a strange, unaccountable Mortal call'd *Jockey Adams*, famous for dancing the *Jockey Dance*, to the Tune of, *Horse to New-Market*. As I was gaping for a Crust, I readily snap'd at the first that offered, and went with this Person to a Town within four Miles of *London*, where a very extraordinary Occurrence happened, and which, had I been really what I represented, might have rid in my own Coach, in the Rear of six Horses.

Notwithstanding my Distresses, the Want of Cloaths was not amongst the Number. I appeared as Mr *Brown*, (A NAME MOST HATEFUL TO ME NOW, FOR REASONS THE TOWN SHALL HAVE SHORTLY LEAVE TO GUESS AT) in a very genteel Manner; and, not making the least Discovery of my Sex by my Behaviour, ever endeavouring to keep up to the well-bred Gentleman, I became, as I may most properly term it, the unhappy Object of Love in a young Lady, whose Fortune was beyond all earthly Power to deprive her of, had it been possible for me

to

to have been, what she designed me, nothing less than her Husband. She was an Orphan Heiress, and under Age, but so near it, that, at the Expiration of eight Months, her Guardian resigned his Trust, and I might have been at once possessed of the Lady, and forty thousand Pounds in the Bank of *England*. Besides Effects in the *Indies*, that were worth about twenty Thousand more.

This was a most horrible Disappointment on both Sides, the Lady of the Husband, and I of the Money, which would have been thought an excellent Remedy for Ills, by those less surrounded with Misery than I was. I, who was the Principal in this Tragedy, was the last acquainted with it. But it got Wind from the Servants, to some of the Players, who, as *Hamlet* says, *Can't keep a Secret*, and they immediately communicated it to me.

Contrary to their Expectation, I received the Information with infinite Concern, not more in regard to myself, than from the poor Lady's Misfortune, in placing her Affection on an improper Object; and whom, by Letters I afterwards received, confirmed me, " *She was too fond of her mistaken Bargain*".

The

The Means by which I came by her Letters, was through the Perswasion of her Maid, who, like most Persons of her Function, are too often ready to carry on Intrigues. 'Twas no difficult Matter to perswade an amorous Heart to follow its own Inclination, and accordingly a Letter came to invite me to drink Tea, at a Place a little distant from the House where she lived.

The Reason given for this Interview was, the Desire some young Ladies of her Acquaintance had to hear me sing, and, as they never went to Plays in the Country, 'twould be a great Obligation to her if I would oblige her Friends, by complying with her Request.

The Maid who brought this Epistle, inform'd of the real Occasion of its being wrote, and told me, if I pleased, I might be happiest Man in the Kingdom, before I was eight and forty Hours older. This frank Declaration from the Servant, gave me but an odd Opinion of the Mistress, and I sometimes conceived, being conscious how unfit I was to embrace so favourable an Opportunity, that it was all a Joke.

However,

However, be it as it might, I resolved to go and know the Reality. The Maid too insisted that I should, and protested her Lady had suffered much on my Account, from the first Hour she saw me, and, but for her, the Secret had never been disclosed. She farther added, I was the first Person who had ever made that Impression on her Mind. I own I felt a tender Concern, and resolved within myself to wait on her, and, by honestly confessing who I was, kill or cure her Hopes of me for ever.

In Obedience to the Lady's Command I waited on her, and found her with two more much of her own Age, who were her Confidents, and entrusted to contrive a Method to bring this Business to an End, by a private Marriage. When I went into the Room I made a general Bow to all, and was for seating myself nearest the Door, but was soon lugg'd out of my Chair by a young Mad-cap of Fashion, and, to both the Lady's Confusion and mine, aukwardly seated by her.

We were exactly in the Condition of Lord *Hardy* and Lady *Charlotte*, in *The Funeral*, and I sat with as much Fear in my Countenance, as if I had stole her Watch from her Side.
She,

She, on her Part, often attempted to speak, but had such a Tremor on her Voice, she ended only in broken Sentences. 'Tis true, I have undergone the dreadful Apprehensions of a Bomb-Bailiff, but I should have thought one at that Time a seasonable Relief, and without repining have gone with him.

The before-mention'd Mad-cap, after putting us more out of Countenance by bursting into a violent Fit of Laughing, took the other by the Sleeve and withdrew, as she thought, to give me a favourable Opportunity of paying my Addresses, but she was deceived, for, when we were alone, I was ten thousand Times in worse Plight than before. And what added to my Confusion was, seeing the poor Soul dissolve into Tears, which she endeavoured to conceal.

This gave me Freedom of Speech, by a gentle Enquiry into the Cause, and, by tenderly trying to sooth her into a Calm, I unhappily encreased, rather than asswaged the dreadful Conflict of Love and Shame which labour'd in her Bosom.

With much Difficulty, I mustered up Courage sufficient to open a Discourse, by which I began to make a Discovery of my

Name

Name and Family, which struck the poor Creature into Astonishment, but how much greater was her Surprize, when I positively assured her that I was actually the youngest Daughter of Mr *Cibber*, and not the Person she conceived me! She was absolutely struck speechless for some little Time, but, when she regained the Power of Utterance, entreated me not to urge a Falshood of that Nature, which she looked upon only as an Evasion, occasioned, she supposed, through a Dislike of her Person. Adding, that her Mind had plainly told her I was no Stranger to her miserable Fate, as she was pleased to term it, and, indeed, as I really thought it.

I still insisted on the Truth of my Assertion, and desired her to consider, whether 'twas likely an indigent young Fellow must not have thought it an unbounded Happiness, to possess at once so agreeable a Lady and immense a Fortune, both which many a Nobleman in this Kingdom would have thought it worth while to take Pains to atchieve.

Notwithstanding all my Arguments, she was hard to be brought into a Belief of what I told her, and conceived that I had taken a Dislike to her, from her too readily consenting to her Servant's making that Declaration of her Passion for me, and, for that Reason, she supposed I had but a light Opinion of her. I assured her of the contrary, and that I was sorry for us both, that Providence had not ordained me to be the happy Person she designed me, that I was much obliged for the Honour she conferr'd on me, and sincerely grieved it was not in my Power to make a suitable Return.

With many Sighs and Tears on her Side, we took a melancholly Leave, and, in a few Days, the Lady retir'd into the Country, where I have never heard from, or of her since, but hope she is made happy in some worthy Husband, that might deserve her.

She was not the most Beautiful I have beheld, but quite the Agreeable, sung finely, and play'd the Harpsichord as well, understood Languages, and was a Woman of real good Sense. But she was, poor Thing! an Instance, in regard to me, *that the Wisest may sometimes err.*

On my Return Home, the Itinerant-Troop all assembled round me, to hear what had passed between the Lady and me ------ when we were to celebrate the Nuptials? ---- Besides many other impertinent, stupid Questions,

some

some offering, agreeable to their villainous Dispositions, as the Marriage they suppos'd would be a Secret, to supply my Place in the Dark, to conceal the Fraud Upon which I look'd at them very sternly, and, with the Contempt they deserved, demanded to know what Action of my Life had been so very monstrous, to excite them to think me capable of one so cruel and infamous?

For the Lady's sake, whose Name I would not for the Universe have had banded about by the Mouths of low Scurrility, I not only told them I had revealed to her who I was, but made it no longer a Secret in the Town, that, in Case it was spoke of, it might be regarded as an Impossibility, or, at worst, a trump'd-up Tale by some ridiculous Blockhead, who was fond of hearing himself prate, as there are indeed too many such. Of which, in Regard to my own Character, I have been often a melancholly Proof, and, as it just now occurs to my Memory, will inform the Reader

As Misfortunes are ever the mortifying Parents of each other, so mine were teeming, and each new Day produced fresh Sorrow. But as if the very Fiends of Destruction were employed to perpetrate mine, and that my
real

real Miseries were not sufficient to crush me with their Weight, a poor, beggarly Fellow, who had been sometimes Supernumerary in *Drury-Lane* Theatre, and Part-writer, forged a most villainous Lye, by saying, I hired a very fine Bay Gelding, and borrowed a Pair of Pistols, to encounter my Father upon *Epping-Forest*, where, I solemnly protest, I don't know I ever saw my Father in my Life That I stopp'd the Chariot, presented a Pistol to his Breast, and used such Terms as I am ashamed to insert, threaten'd to blow his Brains out that Moment, if he did not deliver----- Upbraiding him for his Cruelty in abandoning me to those Distresses he knew I underwent, when he had it so amply in his Power to relieve me: That since he would not use that Power, I would force him to a Compliance, and was directly going to discharge upon him, but his Tears prevented me, and, asking my Pardon for his ill Usage of me, gave me his Purse with threescore Guineas, and a Promise to restore me to his Family and Love, on which I thank'd him, and rode off

A likely Story, that my Father and his Servants were all so intimidated, had it been true, as not to have been able to withstand a single stout Highwayman, much more a Female,

male, and his own Daughter to! However, the Story soon reached my Ear, which did not more enrage me on my own Account, than the impudent, ridiculous Picture the Scoundrel had drawn of my Father, in this supposed horrid Scene. The Recital threw me into such an agonizing Rage, I did not recover it for a Month; but, the next Evening, I had the Satisfaction of being designedly placed where this Villain was to be, and, concealed behind a Screen, heard the Lye re-told from his own Mouth.

He had no sooner ended, than I rushed from my Covert, and, being armed with a thick oaken Plant, knocked him down, without speaking a Word to him; and, had I not been happily prevented should, without the least Remorse, have killed him on the Spot. I had not Breath enough to enquire into the Cause of his barbarous Falshood, but others, who were less concerned than myself, did it for me; and the only Reason he assigned for his saying it, was, *He meant it as a Joke*, which considerably added to the Vehemence of my Rage. But I had the Joy of seeing him well caned, and obliged to ask my Pardon on his Knees----Poor Satisfaction for so manifest an Injury!

This is, indeed, the greatest and most notorious Piece of Cruelty that was ever forged against me, but 'tis a Privilege Numbers have taken with me. and I have generally found, in some Degree or other, my Cause revenged, though by myself unsought And 'tis more than morally possible, I may live to see the Tears of Penitence flow from the Eyes of a yet remaining Enemy, to whose Barbarity I am not the only Victim in the Family. But,

" -----*Come what come may,*
" *Patience and Time run thro' the roughest*
     " *Day*"

If the Person I mean was herself guiltless of Errors, she might "*Stand in some Rank of Praise*" for her Assiduity in searching out the Faults of others, as it might be reasonably supposed the Innocent could never wish to be the Author of Ill to their Fellow-Creatures, and those especially NEARLY ALLIED IN BLOOD We have all Realities of Folly too sufficient to raise a Blush in thinking Minds, without the barbarous Imposition of imaginary ones, which I, and others in the Family, have been cruelly branded with. I shall only give a Hint to
the

the Lady, which I hope she'll prudently observe.

"*The Faults of others we, with Ease,*
   "*discern,*
"*But our own Frailties are the last we*
   "*learn.*"

I shall now give a full Account of, I think, one of the most tragical Occurrences of my Life, which but last Week happened to me. The Reader may remember, in the First Number of my Narrative I made a publick Confession of my Faults, and, pleased with the fond Imagination of being restored to my Father's Favour, flattered myself, e'er this Treatise could be ended, to ease the Hearts of every humane Breast, with an Account of a Reconciliation.

But how FRUITLESS WAS MY ATTEMPT! I wrote, and have thought it necessary, in Justification of my own Character, to print the Letter I sent my Father, who, forgetful of that TENDER NAME, and the GENTLE TIES OF NATURE, returned it me in a blank. Sure that might have been filled up with BLESSING AND PARDON, the only Boon I HOPED FOR, WISHED, OR EX-
PECTED,

PECTED. Can I then be blamed for saying with the expiring *Romeo*,

"------*Fathers have flinty Hearts!* No
" *Tears*
" *Will move 'em!------Children must be*
" *wretched!*

This shocking Circumstance! has since confined me to my Bed, and has been cruelly aggravated by the terrible Reflection of being empowered to say, with *Charles* in *The Fop's Fortune*, " I'm sorry that " I've lost a Father."

I beg Pardon for this Intrusion on the Readers Patience, in offering to their Consideration the following Letter.

To Colley Cibber, *Esq; at his House in Berkly-Square*

Honour'd Sir, Saturday, Mar. 8, 1755.

I Doubt not but you are sensible I last Saturday published the First Number of a Narrative of my Life, in which I made a proper Concession in regard to those unhappy Miscarriages which have for many Years
justly

fi's deprived me of a Father's Fondness. As I am conscious of my Errors, I thought I could not be too publick in suing for your Blessing and Pardon, and only blush to think, my youthful Follies should draw so strong a Compunction on my Mind in the Meridian of my Days, which I might have so easily avoided.

Be assured, Sir, I am perfectly convinced I was more than much to blame, and that the Hours of Anguish I have felt have bitterly repaid me for the Commission of every Indiscretion, which was the unhappy Motive of being so many Years estranged from that Happiness I now, as in Duty bound, most earnestly implore.

I shall, with your Permission, Sir, send again, to know if I may be admitted to throw myself at your Feet, and, with sincere and filial Transport, endeavour to convince you that I am,

HONOUR'D SIR,
  Your truly penitent
    And dutiful Daughter,

      CHARLOTTE CHARKE.

When

When I sent, as is specified in the Letter, for an Answer, I engaged a young Lady, whose tender Compassion was easily moved to be the obliging Messenger. She returned, with friendly Expedition, and delivered me my own Epistle, enclosed in a Blank, from my Father. By the Alteration of my Countenance she too soon perceived the ill Success of her Negotiation, and bore a Part in my Distress.

I found myself so dreadfully disconcerted, I grew impatient to leave my Friend, that I might not intrude too far on her Humanity, which I saw was sensibly affected with my Disappointment. A Disappointment indeed! to be denied that from mortal Man which HEAVEN IS WELL PLEAS'D TO BESTOW, WHEN ADDRESS'D WITH SINCERITY AND PENITENCE, EVEN FOR CAPITAL OFFENCES.

The Prodigal, according to Holy Writ, was joyfully received by the offended Father. Nay, MERCY has even extended itself at the Place of Execution, to notorious Malefactors; but as I have not been guilty of those Enormities incidental to the foremention'd Characters, permit me, gentle Reader, to demand what I have

have done so hateful! so very grievous to his Soul! so much beyond the Reach of Pardon! that nothing but MY LIFE COULD MAKE ATTONEMENT? which I can bring Witness was a Hazard I was immediately thrown into.

THE SHOCK OF RECEIVING MY OWN LETTER did not excite a sudden Gust of unwarrantable Passion, but prey'd upon my Heart with the slow and eating Fire of Distraction and Despair, 'till it ended in a Fever, which now remains upon my Spirits, and which, I fear, I shall find a difficult Task to overcome.

The late Mr *Lillo*'s Character of *Thorowgood*, in his Tragedy of *Barnwell*, sets a beautiful Example of Forgiveness, where he reasonably reflects upon the Frailties of Mankind, in a Speech apart from the afflicted and repenting Youth------" *When we have of-*" *fended Heaven, it requires no more, and* " *shall Man, who needs himself to be for-*" *given, be harder to appease?* "----- Then, turning to the Boy, confirms his Humanity, by saying, " *If my Pardon, or my Love be* " *of Moment to your Peace, look up secure of* " *it.* "

How happy would that last Sentence have made me! as the Want of it has absolutely given me more inexpressible Anguish, than all the accumulated Sorrows I had known before, being now arrived to an Age of Thinking, and well weighing the Consequences arising from the various Occurences of Life. But this, I fear, will prove the heaviest and bitterest Corrosive to my Mind, and the more I reflect on it, find myself less able to support such an Unkindness from that Hand, which, I thought, would have administer'd the gentle Balm of Pity.

I am very certain my Father is to be, in Part, excused, as he is too powerfully perswaded by his cruel Monitor, who neither does, or ever will, pay the least Regard to any Part of the Family, but herself. And though within a Year of Threescore pursues her own Interest, to the Detriment of others, with the same artful Vigilance that might be expected from a young Sharper of Twenty-four. I am certain I have found it so, and am too sure of its Effects from the Hour of my Birth, *and my first Fault, was being my Father's last Born.* Even the little Follies of prattling Infancy were, by this Person, construed in Crimes, before I had a more distinguishing

tinguishing Sense than a Kitten. As I grew up, I too soon perceived a rancourous Disposition towards me, attended with Malice prepense, to destroy that Power I had in the Hearts of both my Parents, where I was perhaps judged to sit too triumphant, and maintained my Seat of Empire in my Mother's to her latest Moments. And, 'tis possible, had she lived, my Enemy might not have carried this cruel Point, to prevent what I think I had a natural Right to receive, when I so earnestly implored it.

One Thing I must insert for her Mortification, that my Conscience is quite serene, and, though she won't suffer my Father to be in Friendship with me, I am perfectly assured that I have, in regard to any Offences towards him, made my Peace with the POWER SUPREME, which neither her Falshood or artful Malice could deprive me of. 'Tis now my Turn to forgive, as being the injured Person; and, to show her how much I chuse to become her Superior in Mind, I not only pardon, but PITY HER. Though, I fear, she rather pursues the Rules observed in the following Lines;

" *Forgiveness*

" *Forgiveness to the Injur'd does belong,*
" *But they ne'er* PARDON, *who have done*
" THE WRONG."

That I have suffered much, is too evidential, and though I neither proposed or expected more than what my Letter expresses, I hope my Father's Eyes, for the sake of his Family who are oppressed, may be one Day opened. For my Part, I cease to think myself belonging to it, and shall conclude this painful Subject with an Assurance to my Brother's two Daughters, That I am sincerely pleased they are so happily provided for, and hope they will have Gratitude and Prudence enough to preserve their Grandsire's Blessing, and never put it in the Power of artful Treachery to elbow them out of his Favour, as I have been, and that most cruelly

I remember the last Time I ever spoke with my Father, a Triumvirate was framed to that End, and I was sent for from the Playhouse to put this base Design in Execution After being baited like a Bull at a Stake, and perceiving they were resolved to carry their horrid Point against me, I grew enraged and obstinate, and, finding a growing Indignation swelling in my Bosom, answered nothing to

their

their Purpose, which incensed my Father Nor can I absolutely blame him, for 'twas undoubtedly my Duty to satisfy any Demand he should think proper to make ----But then again, I considered that his Judgement was sufficient to correct the Errors of my Mind, without the insolent Assistance of those, whose wicked Hearts were fraught with my Ruin

My Father, having been worked up to a strong Fit of Impatience, hastily quitted his House, with a Declaration not to return to it, 'till I was gone. This, I am too well assured,

' *Was a joyful Sound to* Cleopatra's *Ear* "

I staid a few Moments after him, when she, who was once my eldest Sister, was pleased to ask the rest of her Colleagues, if they had done with me, who answering in the Affirmative, in a peremptory Manner turned me out of Doors

I was then married, and had been so near four Years, therefore did not conceive that any one had a Right to treat me like a Child, and could not easily brook being forced into a Submission of that Nature But the main Design was to deprive me of a Birth-right---- and they have done it, for which, in Obedience

ence to the Laws Divine, I beseech Heaven to
forgive them, and bring them to Repentance,
ere it is too late.------And let *Goneril* take
Care, she has found a Brace of *Cordelia*'s in
the Family, which, that they may ever continue, is my heartiest Wish and earnest Prayer
Nor would I have the poor Children think,
because they are made happy, that I envy
them the Advantages they possess No! so
far from it, I am rather delighted than dis-
pleased, as it convinces me my Father has yet
some Power over himself, and, though deaf
to me, has listened to the tender Call of Mercy,
by a seasonable Protection of their Youth and
Innocence

I apprehend I shall be called in Question
for my Inability, in conveying Ideas of the
Passions which most tenderly affect the Heart,
by so often having Recourse to abler Pens
than my own, by my frequent Quotations,
but, in Answer to that, I must beg to be excused, and also justified, as mine and others
Griefs were more strongly painted, by those
Authors I have made bold with, than was
in the Power of my weak Capacity. I thought
there was greater Judgment in such References,
than in vainly attempting to blunder out my
Distress, and possibly, by that Means, tire
the Reader in the Perusal

As

As I have finish'd my tragical Narration, I shall return to the Town, where I was honour'd with the young Lady's Regard. Our Departure from thence happened soon after, and Kings, Queens, Lords and Commons, were all toss'd up in an undistinguished Bundle from that Place, and, like *Sarron*'s Itinerants, escorted to another in a Cart.

As my unlucky Stars were ever employed in working on the Anvil of Misfortune, I, unknowingly, took a Lodging in a Bailiff's House, though not as *Clodio* did, who had three Writs against him, but I was not absolutely certain how long it might be, ere so terrible a Cataſtrophe might be the Cafe, being then but ten Miles from *London*, and every Hour of my Life liable to be seen by some Air-taking Tradesman, to whom, 'twas twenty to one, I might be indebted.

Under such a Circumſtance as this, to be sure, I pass'd my Time mighty pleasingly! but that I might be delivered of the Anxiety and constant Fears that attended me, I perſwaded our Manager (who was under the same unfortunate Circumstance) there was, to my certain Knowledge, a Writ issued out against him, with which he was soon alarmed, and, in order to elude the Hunters, suddenly took away his Company by Night.

I own this was a base Trick, to deprive the Town of the infinite Pleasure they must have received from the incomparable Representations of our sonorous Collection, who, if Noise could plead any Claim to Merit, they were undoubtedly the greatest Proficients of the Age. I have often wondered, that these bawling Heroes do not as tenderly compassionate their Brains, as the Retailers of Flounders in *London* Streets, by an Application of their Hand to one Ear, to preserve the Drum by that necessary Caution.

However, away we went; and, to the great Surprize of the Inhabitants of the next Place we adventur'd to, about Six o'Clock on a *Sunday* Morning we made our Entry, and besieged the Town, but, as our Commander was one of a most intrepid Assurance, he soon fram'd some political Excuses for the Unseasonableness both of the Hour and Day. The Landlord, who happened luckily for us to be an indolent, good-natur'd Man, seeing so large a Company, and such Boxes full of Nothing, come into his House, easily dispensed with the Oddity of our Arrival, and called out lustily for his Maid and Daughter

Daughter to set on the great Pot for the Buttock of Beef, and to make a fine Fire to roast the Loin of Veal. He also ordered the Ostler to help up with the Boxes, which, I own, were weighty, but, I believe, the chief of the Burden consisted of scabbardless, rusty Swords, and departed Mopsticks, transmigrated into Tragedy Truncheons.

For the first Week, we lived like those imaginary Sons of Kings we frequently represented, but, at length, we play'd a Night or two, and no Money coming, upon Enquiry what was for Dinner, the good Host, with an altered Countenance, signified he thought 'twould be better for us to find our own Provision; and apprehending 'twould not do, he advised us to make one good House to pay him, and march off. Upon which one, whose Appetite was extreamly keen, discovered a sudden Paleness, another, enraged at the Disappointment, and feeling the same Demands from Nature, though not equally passive in his Disposition, thundered out a Volley of Oaths, with the Addition of terrible Threats to leave the House, which the Landlord would have been well pleased had he put in Force, and, with a calm Contempt, signified as much.

As I had a Child to support, as well as my unfortunate Self, I thought it highly proper to become a friendly Mediator between these two Persons, and very judiciously introduced myself into farther Credit, by endeavouring to palliate the Matter. But the insensible Puppy, paying more Regard to his offended Honour than his craving Appetite, scolded himself out of the House, and my Daughter and I were continued, by my prudently preserving THE GENTLEMAN, instead of launching into the barbarous Enormities of the BILLINGSGATE HERO.

Business continuing very shocking, I really was ashamed to presume any longer on the partial Regard paid to me by the injur'd Man, and, at last, proposed his using his Interest to put off as many Tickets as he possibly could, in order to make up the several Deficiencies of the Company. This Proposition was kindly accepted, and he soon dispersed a sufficient Number of Tickets to defray all Charges, with many Acknowledgements to me for the Hint, and, that I might not run the Hazard of losing the Reputation I had gain'd, I set off the Day after, well knowing that a

second

second Misfortune of this Nature would not have so happy an End.

With a solitary Shilling I went to *London*, and took a Lodging in about two Hours afterwards at a private House, in *Little Turnstile, Holborn*, but being soon enquired after by another Manager, set out from *London* for *Dartford*, about Three o'Clock in the Afternoon on Foot, in a dreadful Shower of Rain, and reached the Town by Eight in the Evening.

I play'd that Night, for 'tis losing their Charter to begin before Nine or Ten, but my Pumps being thin, and the Rain extream heavy, I contracted such a Hoarseness I was the Day following turn'd off with Half a Crown, and rendered incapable An excellent Demonstration of the Humanity of those low-lived Wretches! who have no farther Regard to the Persons they employ, but while they are immediately serving 'em, and look upon Players like Pack-Horses, though they live by 'em.

When I got to *London*, I had, on Account of my Hoarseness, no View of getting my Bread, as 'twas impossible to hear me speak without a close Application of an Ear to my Mouth. I was then reduced to the Necessity of pledging, from Day to Day, either my own or Child's Cloaths for our Support, and we were stripp'd to even but a bare Change to keep us decently clean, by the Time I began to recover my Voice.

As soon as I was capable of speaking to be heard, I took a second Owl-light Opportunity to seek for Business, and happily succeeded in my Endeavour, and as from Evil often unexpected Good arises, so did it then to me. I went to play a Part in *Gravel-Lane*, where I met with a Woman, who told me she had Scenes and Cloaths in LIMBO for two Guineas, and, if I could propose any Means for their Redemption, she would make me Manager of her Company, if I thought fit to set out with her. I assured her, so far from raising two Guineas, I really did not know where to levy as many Pence, but, in the Night, contemplating on my hapless Fate, I recollected a Friend that I believed would, on Trial, oblige me with that Sum.

To strengthen my Cause, I wrote a Letter as from a Spunging-House, and sent one of the Performers, who had extreamly the Air of a Bomb-Bailiff, to represent that Character

My Friend, moved at my supposed Distress, directly granted my Suit, the Goods were redeemed, and the next Morning we set sail, with a few Hands, for *Gravesend*.

For about a Month we got, one Week with another, a Guinea each Person, from thence we proceeded to *Harwich*, where we met with equal Success for three Weeks more: But unfortunately the Manageress's Husband, who was no Member of the Company, was under Sentence of Transportation in *Newgate*, and she being frequently obliged to pay her Devoirs to her departing Spouse in the dismal Castle of Distress, we broke up, and I returned to *London*.

My projecting Brain was forced again to set itself to work, to find fresh Means of Subsistance, but, for some time, its Labours were ineffectual, 'till even the last Thread of Invention was worn out. At last I resolved to pay circular Visits to my good-natur'd Friends, who redeemed me from the Jaws of Destruction, when under Confinement in *Jackson's-Alley*. I thought the best Excuse I could make for becoming so importunate, was to fix it on a Point of Gratitude, in taking the earliest Opportunity my Circumstances would admit of, to return my sincerest Thanks

for

for so infinite an Obligation, and, after having starved all Day, by the friendly Assistance of the Night, I adventured, and was, by each Person in my several Visits, kindly received, and constantly sent Home with a Means to subsist for sometimes a Day or two; which, as my Circumstances stood, was no small Comfort to one who proceeded in paralytick Order, upon every Excursion

Among the distressful Evening Patroles I made, I one Evening paid my Brother a Visit, who kindly compassionated my Sorrow, and clapping Half a Crown in my Hand, earnestly enjoyned me to dine next Day with him at a Friend's House, who, he knew, had a natural Tendency to Acts of Humanity, and conceived would, in a genteel Manner, be serviceable to me. His good-natur'd Design had the desired Effect, and, in less than three Days I was, by my Brother's Friend, introduced to L---d *A-----a*, who wanted a Gentleman, (being newly come from *I------d*) and nice in regard to the Person he intended for that Office. One well-bred, and who could speak *French*, were two necessary Articles, upon which, Mention was made of me, and an open Declaration who I really was, with a piteous Account of my Misfortunes; which his Lordship very tenderly ly considered, and received me upon the Recommendation of my Brother's Friend.

The Day following I entered into my new Office, which made me the superior Domestick in the Family. I had my own Table, with a Bottle of Wine, and any single Dish I chose for myself, *extra* of what came from my Lord's, and a Guinea paid me every *Wednesday* Morning, that being the Day of the Week on which I entered into his Lordship's Service.

At this Time, my Lord kept in the House with him a *Fille de Joye*. Though no great Beauty, yet infinitely agreeable, (a Native of *Ireland*) remarkably genteel and finely shaped, and a sensible Woman, whose Understanding was embellished by a Fund of good Nature.

When there was any extraordinary Company, I had the Favour of the Lady's at my Table; but, when there was no Company at all, his Lordship permitted me to make a third Person at his, and very good-naturedly obliged me to throw off the Restraint of Behaviour incidental to the Servant, and assume that of the humble Friend and chearful Companion. Many agreeable Evenings I passed in this Manner; and, when Bed-time approached, I took Leave and went Home to my own Lodgings, attending the next Morning at Nine, my appointed Hour

I marched every Day through the Streets with Ease and Security, having his Lordship's Protection, and proud to cock my Hat in the Face of the best of the Bailiffs, and shake Hands with them into the Bargain. In this State of Tranquility I remained for about five Weeks, when, as the Devil would have it, there came two supercilious Coxcombs, who, wanting Discourse and Humanity, hearing that I was his Lordship's Gentleman, made me their unhappy Theme, and took the Liberty to arraign his Understanding for entertaining one of an improper Sex in a Post of that Sort. His Lordship's Argument was, for a considerable Time, supported by the Strength of his Pity for an unfortunate Wretch, who had never given him the least Offence. But the pragmatical Blockheads teized him at last into a Resolution of discharging me the next Day, and I was once again reduced to my Scenes of Sorrow and Desolation.

I must do Justice to the Peer, to confess he did not send me away empty handed, but so small a Pittance as he was pleased to bestow, was little more than a momentary Support for myself and Child. When my small Stock was exhausted, I was most terribly puzzled for a Recruit.

Friendship began to cool! Shame encompassed me! that where I had the smallest Hope of Redress remaining, I had not Courage sufficient to make an Attack. In short, Life became a Burden to me, and I began to think it no Sin not only to WISH, but even DESIRE to die. When Poverty throws us beyond the Reach of Pity, I can compare our Beings to nothing so adaptly, as the comfortless Array of tattered Garments in a frosty Morning.

But Providence, who has ever been my Friend and kind Director, as I was in one of my Fits of Despondency, suddenly gave a Check to that Error of my Mind, and wrought in me a Resolution of making a bold Push, which had but two Chances, either for my Happiness or Destruction----Which is as follows.

I took a neat Lodging in a Street facing *Red-Lyon-Square*, and wrote a Letter to Mr *Beard*, intimating to him the sorrowful Plight I was in, and, in a Quarter of an Hour

Hour after, my Request was most obligingly complied with by that worthy Gentleman, whose Bounty enabled me to set forward to *Newgate-Market*, and bought a considerable Quantity of Pork at the best Hand, which I converted into Sausages, and with my Daughter set out, laden with each a Burden as weighty as we could well bear; which, not having been used to Luggages of that Nature, we found extreamly troublesome. But *Necessitas non habeat Leges*----We were bound to that, or starve.

Thank Heaven, our Loads were like *Æsop*'s when he chose to carry the Bread, which was the weightiest Burden, to the Astonishment of his Fellow-Travellers; not considering that his Wisdom preferred it, because he was sure it would lighten as it went. So did ours, for as I went only where I was known, I soon disposed, among my Friends, of my whole Cargo, and was happy in the Thought, that the utmost Excesses of my Misfortunes had no worse Effect on me, than an industrious and honest Inclination to get a small Livelihood, without Shame or Reproach. Though the Arch-Dutchess of our Family, who would not have relieved me with a Half-penny Roll or a Draught of Small-Beer, imputed this to me as a Crime.

I suppose

I suppose she was possessed with the same dignified Sentiments Mrs *Peachum* is endowed with, and THOUGHT THE HONOUR OF THEIR FAMILY WAS CONCERNED If so, she knew the way to have prevented the Disgrace, and in a humane, justifiable Manner, have preserved her own from that Taint of Cruelty I doubt she will never overcome

My being in Breeches was alledged to me as a very great Error, but the original Motive proceeded from a particular Cause, and I rather chuse to undergo the worst Imputation that can be laid on me on that Account, than unravel the Secret, which is an Appendix to one I am bound, as I before hinted, by all the Vows of Truth and Honour everlastingly to conceal.

For some Time I subsisted as a Higgler, with tolerable Success, and, instead of being despised by those who had served me in my utmost Exigencies, I was rather applauded. Some were tender enough to mingle their pitying Tears, with their Approbation of my endeavouring at an honest Livelihood, as I did not prostitute my Person, or use any other indirect Means for Support, that might have

have brought me to Contempt and Disgrace.

Misfortunes, to which all are liable, are too often the Parents of Forgetfulness and Disregard in those we have, in happier Times, obliged. Too sure I found it so! for I could name many Persons, who are still in Being, that I have both clothed and fed, who have since met with Success, but when strong Necessity reduced me to an Attempt of using their Friendship, scarce afforded me a civil Answer, which closed in an absolute Denial, and consequently the Sting of Disappointment on such Occasions struck the deeper to my Heart. Though none so poignant, as the Rebuffs I met with from those who ought, in regard to themselves, to have prevented my being under such universal Obligations, but, instead of acting agreeable to the needful Sentiments of Compassion and sorrowful Regret, for the Sufferings of a near Relation, where a villainous Odium could not be thrown a ridiculous one was sure to be cast, even on the innocent Actions of my Life.

Upon being met with a Hare in my Hand, carried by Order to the Peer I had then lately lived with, this single Creature was enumerated

rated into a long Pole of Rabbits, and 'twas affirmed as a Truth, that I made it my daily Practice to cry them about the Streets.

This Falshood was succeeded by another, that of my selling Fish, an Article I never thought of dealing in, but notwithstanding, the wicked Forger of this Story positively declared, that I was selling some Flounders one Day, and, seeing my Father, stept most audaciously up to him, and slapt one of the largest I had full in his Face. Who, that has common Senses, could be so credulous to receive the least Impression from so inconsistent a Tale; or that, if it had been true, if I had escaped my Father's Rage, the Mob would not, with strictest Justice, have prevented my surviving such an unparallel'd Villainy one Moment?

I always thought myself unaccountable enough in Reality, to excite the various Passions of Grief and Anger, Pity or Contempt, without unnecessary additional Falshoods to aggravate my Misdeeds. I own I was obliged, 'till seiz'd with a Fever, to trudge from one Acquaintance to another with Pork and Poultry, but never had the Honour of being a Travelling-fishmonger, nor the
Villainy

Villainy of being guilty of that infamous Crime I was inhumanly charged with.

When I was brought so low, by my Illness, as to be disempowered to carry on my Business myself, I was forced to depend upon the infant Industry of my poor Child; whose Strength was not able to bear an equal Share of Fatigue, so that I consequently was obliged to suffer a considerable Deficiency, by the Neglect of my Customers: And though I could scarce afford myself the least Indulgence, in regard to my Illness, I found, though in a trifling Degree, it largely incroached upon my slender Finances, so that I was reduced to my last three Pounds of Pork, nicely prepared for Sausages, and left it on the Table covered up As I was upon Recovery, I took it in my Head a little fresh Air would not be amiss, and set forth into *Red-Lyon-Fields* But, on my Return, OH! DISASTROUS CHANCE! a hungry Cur had most savagely entered my Apartment, confounded my Cookery, and most inconsiderately devoured my remaining Stock, and, from that Hour, a Bankruptcy ensued! the Certificate of which was signed, by the Woefulness of my Countenance at the horrid View.

The

The Child and I gap'd and star'd at each other, and, with a Despondency in our Faces, very natural on so deplorable an Occasion, we sat down and silently conceived that starving must be the sad Event of this shocking Accident, having at that Time neither Meat, Money, nor Friends. My Week's Lodging was up the next Day, and I was very sure of a constant Visit from my careful Landlord, but how to answer him was a puzzling Debate *between me and myself*, and I was very well assured, could only be answered but by an Affirmative in that Point.

After having sighed away my Senses for my departed Pork, I began to consider that Sorrow would not retrieve my Loss, or pay my Landlord, and without really knowing where to go, or to whom I should apply, I walked out 'till I should either meet an Acquaintance, or be inspired with some Thought that might happily draw off the Scene of Distress I was then immers'd in.

Luckily, I met with an old Gentlewoman whom I had not seen many Years, and who knew me when I was a Child. She, perceiving Sadness in my Aspect, enquired into the Cause of that, and my being in Mens Cloaths,

Cloaths, which, as far as I thought proper, I informed her When we parted, she slipt Five Shillings into my Hand, on which I thankfully took Leave, went Home with a chearful Heart, paid my Lodging off next Morning, and quitted it.

The next Vexation that arose, was how to get another, for the Child was too young to be sent on such an Errand, and I did not dare to make my Appearance too openly. However, that Grief was soon solved by the good Nature of a young Woman, who gave a friendly Invitation to us both, and, though not in the highest Affluence, supported myself and Child for some Time, without any View or Hopes of a Return, which has since established a lasting Friendship between us, as I received more Humanity from her Indigence, than I could obtain even a Glimpse of from those, whose FORTUNES I had a more ample Right to expect a Relief from.

I had not been many Days with my Friend before I relapsed, my Fever encreasing to that Degree my Death was hourly expected, and, being deprived of my Senses, was left without Means of Help in this unhappy Situation, and, had it not been for the extensive Goodness of the Person before-mentioned, my

Child

Child must have either begged her Bread, or perished for the Want of it.

When I was capable of giving a rational Answer, she was my first Care; and I had, in the Midst of this Extremity, the pleasing Relief of being informed, my Friend's Humanity had protected her from that Distress I apprehended she must have otherwise suffered, from the Severity of my Illness. I was incapable of writing, and therefore sent a verbal Message, by my good Friend, to my Lord A-----a, who sent me a Piece of Gold, and expressed a tender Concern for my Misfortunes and violent Indisposition.

As soon as I was able to crawl, I went to pay my Duty there, and was again relieved through his Bounty, and might have returned to my Place, 'till something else had fallen out, but that his Lordship was obliged to go suddenly out of *England*, which, as I had a Child, was not suitable to either him or me.

Mr *Yeates*'s New Wells being open, and he having Occasion for a Singer in the Serious Part of an Entertainment, called, *Jupiter and Alcmena*, I was sent for to be his *Mercury*, and, by the Time that was ready
for

for Exhibition, I began to be tolerably recovered. And a Miracle indeed it was, that I overcame a dreadful Spotted-Fever, without the Help of Advice. Nor had I any Remedy applied, except an Emetick, prescribed and sent me by my Sister *Marples*, who was the only Relation I had that took any Notice of me.

As I have no Power of making her Amends, equal to my Inclinations, I can only entreat the Favour of my Acquaintance in general, and those whom I have not the Pleasure of knowing, whenever 'tis convenient and agreeable for them to use a neat, well accommodated House of Entertainment, they will fix a lasting Obligation on me by going to her's, which she opened last *Thursday*, the 20th Instant, in *Fullwood's-Rent*, near *Gray's-Inn*: Where they will be certain of Flesh, Fish and Poultry, dressed in an elegant Manner, at reasonable Rates, good Wines, &c and a Politeness of Behaviour agreeable to the Gentlewoman; whose hard Struggles, through Seas of undeserved Misfortunes, will, I hope, be a Claim to that Regard I am certain she deserves, and will, wherever she finds it, most gratefully acknowledge.

Fo-

For some few Months I was employed, as before-mentioned, 'till *Bartholomew* Fair; and, as I thought 'twould be more advantageous to me to be there, obtained Leave of Mr. *Yeates* to quit the Wells for the four Days, and returned to him at the Expiration thereof.

The Rumour of my being in Business having spread itself among my Creditors, I was obliged to decamp; being too well assured my small Revenue, which was but just sufficient to buy Bread and Cheese, would not protect me from a Jail, or satisfy their Demands. Had not my Necessities been pressing, my Service would not have been purchased at so cheap a Rate; but thought I must have been everlastingly condemned, had I, through Pride, been so repugnant to the Laws of Nature, Reason and maternal Love, as to have rejected, with insolent Scorn, this scanty Maintainance, when I was conscious I had not Sixpence in the World to purchase a Loaf. I therefore found it highly necessary to set apart the Remembrance of what I had been,

" I THEN WAS WHAT I HAD MADE MY-
" SELF;"

And, consequently, obliged to submit to every Inconvenience of Life my Misfortunes could possibly involve me in.

The Amount of all I owed in the World did not arise to Five and Twenty Pounds, but I was as much perplexed for that Sum as if it had been as many Thousands. In order to secure my Person and defend myself from Want, I joined with a Man who was a Master of Legerdemain, but, on my entering on an Agreement with him, he commenced Manager, and we tragedized in a Place called *Petticoat-Lane*, near *White-Chapel*, I then taking on me THAT DARLING NAME OF BROWN, which was a very great Help to my Concealment, and indeed the only ADVANTAGE I EVER RECEIVED FROM IT, OR THOSE WHO HAVE A BETTER CLAIM TO IT

But to my Purpose. I soon grew tired of leading such a Life of Fear, and resolved to make Trial of the Friendship of my late Uncle, and wrote a melancholly Epistle to him, earnestly imploring his Assistance, for the sake of his deceased Sister (my dear Mother) to give me as much Money as would be necessary to set me up in a Publick House I told him, I would not put it upon the Foot of borrowing, as 'twas ten Millions to one whether

ther he might ever be repaid, and, in Case of Failure of a Promise of that Nature, I knew I must of Course be subject to his Displeasure, therefore fairly desired him to make it a Gift, if he thought my Circumstances worthy his Consideration, which, to do him Justice, indeed he did, and ordered me to take a House directly, that he might be assured of the Sincerity of my Intention.

I obeyed his Commands the next Day, and, as I have been in a Hurry from the Hour of my Birth, precipitately took the first House where I saw a Bill, and which, unfortunately for me, was in *Drury-Lane*, that had been most irregularly and indecently kept by the last Incumbent, who was a celebrated Dealer in murdered Reputations, Wholesale and Retale.

This I, through a natural Inadvertency, never considered, nor what ill Consequences must reasonably attend so imprudent a Choice of my Situation. Choice I can't properly call it, for I really did not give myself Time to make one, 'twas sufficient that I had a House, and rattled away, as fast as a Pair of Horses could gallop, to inform my Uncle *how charmingly I was fixed*

He, according to his Word, gave me a Bank-Note directly, and a Sum of Money in Gold besides. Providence was merciful enough to afford me a decent Quantity of Patience to stay long enough to thank him, in that respectful Manner which Duty obliged me to, and his Bounty truly deserved; but, I remember, as soon as I got into the Coach, I began to think the Happiness I then enjoyed to be too great, and too substantial to be true.

Having been so long the Slave of Misery! and Child of Sorrow! it appeared to me like a Dream, and I was in *Nell Jobson*'s Condition on that Score, who never wished, from a Surmise of exactly the same Kind, ever to wake again. I had not Patience to go Home, but stopped at a Tavern to count my Money, and read my Note as often, I believe, as there were Shillings in every separate Pound, 'till o' my Conscience I had enumerated every Shilling, in Imagination, to a Pound.

The first Thing I did, was to hasten to my principal Creditor, who, by the Bye, had issued out a Writ against me a Month before, but was, through a fruitless Search, obliged to drop his Action; though really the Man was so good-natured, as to hope I would consider

sider the Expences he had been at on that Account, and that not finding me had put him to a supernumerary Charge, which I was undoubtedly strangely obliged to him for! As a Proof how much I thought myself so, I begged the Favour of him to give me a Receipt for the Money, and when he could prevail upon a reprieved Criminal to pay for the erecting of *Tyburn* Tree, because he was not hanged there, he should be perfectly assured of all Costs he had been at, in tenderly endeavouring to confine me in a Prison.

The Chap, I believe, was glad of his Money, but cursedly vexed he had not staid 'till the Report of an Amendment of my Circumstances, which would have run me to an equal Expence of the Debt, thro' the unnecessary Charges *the dear Man* would have put me to.

When I had given this "CERBERUS "A SOP," I flew, with impatient Joy, to all the Brokers in Town, to buy my Houshold Furniture, gave the asking Price for every Thing I bought, and, in less than three Hours, my House was thoughtlessly furnished, with many Things I had no real Occasion for.

I dare answer for it, that some *delicate old Maid or prudent Wife*, will bless themselves at this strange Recital; and, with vacant, up-lifted Eyes, thank Heaven I was no Relation of theirs *That they* did not wonder such an inconsiderate *Wretch should be so unhappy!* When, poor Devils! the same Fate would have drawn equal Incumbrances upon their Gravities, and perhaps without the Advantage of Spirits to surmount them, as I have done, for which,

THANK HEAVEN ALONE.

I hope, as I have been often DESERVEDLY, and sometimes UNDESERVEDLY the Motive of Laughter in others, I may be allowed to come in for my Share, and beg Leave to inform the Town, That I can as heartily join with them in that Respect as they could wish, and more than they may probably expect.

But this Affair was attended with such numerous UNACCOUNTABLE Proceedings, I can't blame any Body for being thrown into a speechless Astonishment. As for Example ---- As soon as I had cluttered an undistinguishable Parcel of Goods into my House,

House, which was after the Hour of Five in the Evening, I resolved to lie there that Night. Beds were to be put up, and every Thing ranged in proper Order. By the Time these Matters were accomplished, I was forced to forgoe my Resolution of sleeping there that Night, it being near Six in the Morning before I could advance to my Repository Where, when I was imagined to take my Rest, my impatient and elevated Spirits would not let me continue 'till the reasonable Hour of rising throughout the Neighbourhood, but, through Excess of Joy, I arose, and contrived fresh Means to unlade me of Part of the Treasure my Uncle had possessed me of.

I dare venture to affirm, I had not been two Days and a Half in the House before 'twas open'd, and, as is customary on such Occasions, gave away an Infinity of Ham, Beef and Veal, to every Soul who came and call'd for a Quart of Beer, or a single Glass of Brandy. The Faces of many of them I never saw before or since, but was, from the Number of People that came the *first Day, fully convinced, that I should carry on a roaring Trade* Though I afterwards found, I had successfully run myself out very near seven Pounds, in less than twenty-four Hours, to acquire, *nothing at all.*

The

The next great Help I had towards getting an Estate, was the Happiness of the unprofitable Custom of several Strolling-Actors, who were unfortunately out of Business; and, tho' they had no Money, I thought it incumbent on me, as they stil'd themselves Comedians, to credit them 'till they got something to do. Not considering, when that happened, they might in all Probability be many score Miles out of my Reach, which indeed proved to be the very Case.

Another Expedient, towards the making my Fortune, was letting three several Rooms to as many different Persons, but in Principle were all alike, and conjunctive in the Perpetration of my Destruction, which I shall define in few Words. One of the Party has very narrowly escaped hanging, more from Dint of Mercy than Desert. Another reduced to common Beggary, and lying on Bulks; being so notorious a Pilferer, as to be refused Admittance into the most abject, tottering Tenement in or about St *Giles*'s And the third is transported for Life.

Very unfortunately for me the Water was laid into my Cellar, and I having no Design of doing Injuries, suspected none; but found, too

too late, that my Tap had run faster than the Water-Cock, and my Beer carried in Pails to the two Pair of Stairs and Garrets, which too frequently set the House in an Uproar, as the Gentry, at poor *Pilgarlick*'s Expence, got themselves excessive drunk, and constantly quarrell'd. Insomuch, that they began at length to impeach one another, by distant Hints and Winks, assuring me, that they believed 'twould be very proper to observe Mrs *Such-a-one*, when she went about the House, what she carried up Stairs. Presently the Person of whom I was warned would come to me, and give the same Caution of the other, and, in Half an Hour's Time, the Husbands of these People would come and do the same by each other.

These Hints made me begin to be a little peery, and resolved to look round the House to see if any Thing was missing. In short, they had taken violent Fancies to my very Candlesticks and Sauce-pans, my Pewter terribly shrunk, and my Coals daily diminished, from the same Opportunity they had in conveying off my Beer; and, as I kept an Eating-House also, there was very often a Hue and Cry after an imaginary Dog, that had run away with three Parts of a Joint of Meat.

As

As my Stock was thus daily and cruelly impaired, consequently my Profits were not able to make up for the horrid Deficiency, and, as I did not dare to make a second Attempt on my Uncle, I prudently resolved to throw up my House, before I run myself into such Inconveniencies, by endeavouring to keep it, I might not easily have overcome. So suddenly disrob'd my own Apartments of their Furniture, and quitted 'em, on which the thieving Crew were then obliged to disperse, being deprived of all future Hopes of making me thus inhumanly their Prey.

I must beg Pardon of the Reader for omitting a Circumstance, that happened about a Year before I was thus intendedly settled by my Uncle. Being, as I frequently was, in great Distress, I went to see a Person who knew me from my Childhood, and though not in a Capacity of serving me beyond their good Wishes and Advice, did their utmost to convince me, as far as that extended, how much they had it at Heart to serve me; and, upon Enquiry into what Means I proposed for a Subsistance, I gave the good Woman to understand there was nothing, which did not exceed the Bounds of Honesty, that I should think unworthy of my undertaking: That I had

had been so innur'd to Hardships of the Mind, I should think those of the Body rather a kind Relief, if they would afford but daily Bread for my poor Child and Self.

The Woman herself knew who I was, but her Husband was an entire Stranger, to whom she introduced me as a young Gentleman of a decay'd Fortune, and, after apoligizing for Half an Hour, proposed to her Spouse to get me the Waiter's Place, which was just vacant, at one Mrs *Dorr*'s, who formerly kept the *King's-Head*, at *Mary-la-Bonne*.

I thankfully accepted the Offer, and went the next Morning to wait on the Gentlewoman, introduced by my Friend's Husband, and neither he or Mrs *Dorr* in the least suspected who I was. She was pleased to tell me, she liked me on my first Appearance; but was fearful, as she understood I was well born and bred, that her Service would be too hard for me. Perceiving me to wear a melancholly Aspect, tenderly admonished me to seek out for some less robust Employment, as she conjectur'd that I should naturally lay to Heart the Impertinence I must frequently be liable to, from the lower Class of People; who, when in their Cups, pay no Regard either to Humanity or good Manners.

I began

I began to be Half afraid, her Concern would make her talk me from my Purpose, and, not knowing which Way to dispose of myself, begg'd her not to be under the least Apprehensions of my receiving any Shock on that Account. That notwithstanding I was not born to Servitude, since Misfortunes had reduced me to it, I thought it a Degree of Happiness, that a mistaken Pride had not foolishly possessed me with a Contempt of getting an honest Livelihood, and chusing rather to perish by haughty Penury, than prudently endeavour to forget what I had been, and patiently submit to the Severities of Fortune, which, at that Time, was not in my Power to amend.

To be short, the Gentlewoman bore so large a Share in my Affliction, she manifested her Concern by a hearty Shower of Tears, and, as she found I was anxious for a Provision with her, we agreed, and the next Day I went to my Place. But when I informed her I had a Daughter about ten Years of Age, she was doubly amazed; and the more so, to hear a young Fellow speak so feelingly of a Child.

She ask'd me, if my Wife was living? I told her no; that she died in Child-Bed
of

of that Girl, whom she insisted should be brought to see her next Day, and entertained the poor Thing in a very genteel Manner, and greatly compassionated her's and her supposed Father's Unhappiness.

I was the first Waiter that was ever permitted to sit at Table with her; but, she was pleased to compliment me, that she thought my Behaviour gave me a Claim to that Respect, and that 'twas with the utmost Pain she obliged herself to call me any Thing but, Sir.

To her great Surprize, she found me quite a handy Creature, and being light and nimble, trip'd up and down Stairs with that Alacrity of Spirit and Agility of Body, that is natural to those Gentlemen of the Order of the Tap-tub, though, as *Hob* says, we sold all Sorts of Wine and Punch, &c.

At length *Sunday* came, and I began to shake in my Shoes, for fear of a Discovery, well knowing our House to be one of very great Resort, as I found it, for I waited that Day upon twenty different Companies, there being no other Appearance of a Male, except myself, throughout the House, exclusive of the Customers, and, to my violent

Astonishment, not one Soul among 'em all that knew me.

Another Recommendation of me to my good Mistress, was my being able to converse with the Foreigners, who frequented her Ordinary every Sabbath-Day, and to whom she was unable to talk, but by Signs, which I observing, prevented her future Trouble, by signifying in the *French* Tongue, I perfectly well understood it. This was a universal Joy round the Table, which was encompassed by *German* Peruke-Makers and *French* Taylors, not one of whom could utter one single Syllable of *English*.

As soon as Mrs *Dorr* heard me speak *French*, away she run with her Plate in her Hand, and, laughing, left the Room to go down and eat an *English* Dinner, having, as she afterwards told me, been obliged once a Week to dine pantomimically, for neither she or her Company were able to converse by any other Means.

When I came down with the Dishes, I thought the poor Soul would have eat me up, and sent as many thankful Prayers to Heaven as would have furnished a Saint for a Twelvemonth in Behalf of the Man who
brought

brought me to her. Her over-Joy of her Deliverance from her foreign Companions, wrought a generous Effect on her Mind; which I had a convincing Proof of, by her presenting me with Half a Crown, and made many Encomiums I thought impossible for me ever, in such a Sphere of Life, to be capable of deserving.

In regard to my Child, I begg'd not to be obliged to lie in the House, but constantly came to my Time in a Morning, and staid 'till about Ten or Eleven at Night, and have often wondered I have escaped, without Wounds or Blows, from the Gentlemen of the Pad, who are numerous and frequent in their Evening Patroles through them Fields, and my March extended as far as *Long-Acre*, by which Means I was obliged to pass through the thickest of 'em. But Heaven everlastingly be praised! I never had any Encounter with 'em, and used to jog along with the Air of a raw, unthinking, pennyless 'Prentice, which I suppose, rendered me not worthy their Observation.

In the Week Days, Business (though good,) was not so very brisk as on *Sundays*, so that when I had any leisure Hours I employed 'em in working in the Garden, which I was then capable

capable of doing with some small Judgment, but that, and every Thing else, created fresh Surprize in my Mistress, who behaved to me as if I had been rather her Son than her Servant.

One Day, as I was setting some *Windsor* Beans, the Maid came to me, and told me she had a very great Secret to unfold, but that I must promise never to tell that she had discovered it. As I had no extraordinary Opinion of her Understanding, or her Honesty, I was not over anxious to hear this mighty Secret, lest it should draw me into some Premunire, but she insisted upon disclosing it, assuring me 'twas something that might turn to my Advantage, if I would make a proper Use of it. This last Assertion raised in me a little Curiosity, and I began to grow more attentive to her Discourse; which ended in assuring me, to her certain Knowledge, I might marry her Mistress's Kinswoman, if I would pay my Addresses, and that she should like me for a Master extreamly, advising me to it by all Means.

I asked her what Grounds she had for such a Supposition? To which she answer'd, she had Reasons sufficient for what she had said, and I was the greatest Fool in the World

Mrs. Charlotte Charke. 163

World if I did not follow her Advice. I positively assured her I would not, for I would not put it in the Power of a Mother-in-Law to use my Child ill, and that I had so much Regard, as I pretended, to the Memory of her Mother, I resolved never to enter into Matrimony a second Time.

Whatever was the Motive, I am entirely ignorant of, but this insensible Mortal had told the young Woman, that I intended to make Love to her, which, had I really been a Man, would have never entered in my Imagination, for she had no one Qualification to recommend her to the Regard of any Thing beyond a Porter or a Hackney-Coachman. Whether she was angry at what I said to the Wench, in regard to my Resolution against marrying, or whether it was a Forgery of the Maid's, of and to us both, I cannot positively say, but a Strangeness ensued, and I began to grow sick of my Place, and stay'd but a few Days after.

In the Interim Somebody happened to come, who hinted that I was a Woman, upon which, Madam, to my great Surprize, attacked me with insolently presuming to say she was in Love with me, which I assured her I never had the least Conception of. *No, truly, I believe,*

believe, said she, *I should hardly be 'namour'd* WITH ONE OF MY OWN SEX Upon which I burst into a Laugh, and took the Liberty to ask her, if she understood what she said? This threw the offended Fair into an absolute Rage, and our Controversy lasted for some Time; but, in the End, I brought in Vindication of my own Innocence, the Maid to Disgrace, who had uncalled for trumped up so ridiculous a Story.

'Mrs *Dorr* still remained incredulous, in regard to my being a Female; and though she afterwards paid me a Visit, with my worthy Friend (at my House in *Drury-Lane*) who brought my unsuccessful Letter back from my Father, she was not to be convinced, I happening that Day to be in the Male-Habit, on Account of playing a Part for a poor Man, and obliged to find my own Cloaths.

She told me, she wished she had known me better when I lived with her, she would, on no Terms, have parted with her Man *Charles*, as she had been informed I was capable of being Master of the Ceremonies, in managing and conducting the Musical Gardens, for she had a very fine Spot of Ground, calculated entirely for that Purpose, and would have trusted the Care of it to my Government

ment. But 'twas then too late; which I am sorry for, on the Gentlewoman's Account, who might have been by such a Scheme preserved in her House, from which, through ill Usage, in a short Time after she was drove out, and reduced to very great Extremities, even by those most nearly related to her *But I find 'tis become a fashionable Vice, to proclaim War against those we ought to be most tender of; and the surest and only Way to find a Friend, is to make a Contract with the greatest Stranger.*

After I left my unfortunate Mistress, I was obliged to look out for Acting-Jobbs, and luckily one soon presented itself. One Mr. *Scudamore*, a Serjeant of Dragoons, who had been some Years before a Player, on his Return from Battle (where our Royal Youthful Hero had immortalized his Fame in his Father's and Country's Defence) took *The Recruiting Officer* for his Benefit, played Capt. *Plume*, and engaged me for *Sylvia*, and also to write him a Prologue on the Occasion, which he spoke himself.

I don't pretend to have any extraordinary Talents, in regard to Poetry in Verse, or indeed in Prose, but as it speaks the Warmth of my Heart towards the Royal Family, whose illustrious

illustrious Line may Heaven to latest Posterity extend, I will venture to insert what I wrote. And hope, though I am but an insignificant and humble Subject, every true *Briton* will let my Zeal plead an Excuse for my Deficiency, in the attempting so noble and glorious a Theme.

From Toils and Dangers of a furious War,
Where Groans and Death successive wound the Air,
Where the fair Ocean, or the chrystal Flood,
Are dy'd with purple Streams of flowing Blood,
I am once more, thank Providence, restor'd,
'Tho' narrowly escap'd, the Bullet and the Sword
Amidst the sharpest Terrors I have stood,
And smil'd at Tumults, for my Country's Good.
But where's the Briton dare at Fate repine?
When our Great WILLIAM's *foremost of the Line!*
With steady Courage dauntless he appears,
And owns a Spirit far beyond his Years
With Wisdom, as with Justice, he spurr'd on,
To save this Nation from a Papal Throne.

May

*May gracious Heav'n the youthful Hero give,
Long smiling Years of Happiness to live
And Britons, with united Voices, sing,
The noblest Praises of their glorious King,
Who, to defend his Country and its Rights,
Parted from him in whom his Soul delights.
Then, with a grateful Joy, Britannia own,
NONE BUT GREAT GEORGE SHOULD FILL THE BRITISH THRONE*

Though my Poetry may be lame, my Design was good, and, as I am sensible it has no other Merit than that, shall say no more about it, but that it was well received at the *Hay-Market* Theatre, and I was handsomely rewarded by the Person whose Benefit it was wrote for.

I must acknowledge the Story of my Situation at *Mary-la-Bonne* is not properly ranged in my History, according to the Time it happened, but, as it made up the Number of my Oddities, I have made bold to hawl it in, as I think it is as remarkable as any other Part of my Life before-mentioned.

After I left my House (which my Uncle's kind Pail of Milk enabled me to go into, though soon after kicked down by his ridiculous Marriage) I went to the *Hay-Market*, where my Brother revived the Tragedy of *Romeo and Juliet*, and would have succeeded by other Pieces he got up, in particular by the Run of *Cymbeline*, but was obliged to desist by Virtue of an Order from the L--- -d C--------n. I imagine, partly occasioned by a Jealousy of his having a Likelihood of a great Run of the last-mentioned Play, and which would of Course been detrimental, in some Measure, to the other Houses

While we were permitted to go on my Brother and I lived together, where I passed my Time both chearfully and agreeably And 'tis no Compliment, to own the Pleasure and Advantage I reaped from his daily Conversation, was the Foundation of that pleasing Content I enjoyed, whilst he was a Resident at that Theatre.

But as my Happiness was never of very long Duration, my Brother was invited, on the Suppression, to *Covent-Garden* Theatre, and I was left to make the best I could, with the remaining Few who had a Mind to try their
Fortunes

Fortunes with me: And indeed, to do my Brother Justice, he promised me I should have the Advantage of his Daughter *Jenny*'s Performance, as I was left suddenly, and in Distress.

As she was a promising Actress in a tender, soft Light, I designed to set her forth to the best Advantage, and there was nothing wanting but her Father's Presence to carry every Thing on as orderly as before. Though his going was the only Means that rendred it practicable for me to keep the House open, for, when he was removed,

"*We did our Safety to our Weakness one,*
"*As Grass escapes the Scythe by being*
"*low.*"

Yet I was determined, had my Niece remained with me, to have been as industrious as possible, both for her Sake and my own, and, as I had appeared in some first Characters, was resolved to endeavour at filling up all those, with which she was most concerned, as our Figures were agreeably match'd, I being but of the Bulk and Stature of most of our modern fine Gentlemen, and Miss *Jenny*, who was a growing Girl of Sixteen, exactly tally'd with me in that Respect.

When

When my Brother governed the Theatre, he got up *The Conscious Lovers*, which we play'd four Nights succeffively, to full Houfes, in which I appear'd in the Character of Young *Bevil*, the Child in *Indiana*, and her Father in *Tom*.

As I had been not only endured, but really well received in fuch a Part, during my Brother's Reign, I could not conceive that his throwing up the Reins of Empire could leffen me in the Efteem of the good-natur'd Part of the Town, who had been kind enough to afford me, perhaps, more than my Share of Applaufe: But 'twas otherwife thought by fome of my DEAR FRIENDS, who prevailed on my Father to fend his pofitive Commands to his Son to withdraw his Daughter, on Pain of his Difpleafure.

I was then reviving an old Play, call'd, *Pope Joan*, in which I afterwards exhibited that Character, to a dreadful Houfe, which I partly attribute to being deprived of my Niece, who was to have performed the Part of *Angeline*. When the Bills were up, and her Name not there, all thofe who were fond of feeing and encouraging her growing Genius, fent back their Tickets, with various Excufes for their Non-Attendance, and 'twas debated in the Family, *'Twould be a Scandal for her to play with such a Wretch as I was* *'Twas letting her down, to be seen with me, as her Father was not there to keep her in Countenance.*

I should be glad to know, what mighty Degree of theatrical Dignity the harmless Child was possessed of preferable to myself, as a Player? I was, when even under Age, received in capital Characters at *Drury-Lane*, where I made my first Appearance, and in such Parts, my riper Judgment makes me tremble to think I had, only with an uncultivated Genius, Courage enough to undertake

In regard to her Birth, I presume I was upon a Par with her, as her Grandfather's Daughter, and her Father's Sister *The only Disgrace was, my being under Misfortunes, the very worst Reason for my Family's contributing to a Perpetration of that, which Nature and Humanity should rather have excited 'em to have helped me to overcome*

In respect to an Improvement in her Business, I was thought worthy of instructing her in the Part of *Indiana*, which another of her

Aunts

Aunts can testify the Truth of, who came with her into my own Apartment several Days for that Purpose

I suppose the Reason of an Application to me on that Account, proceeded from my Brother's Hurry of Business, which prevented his doing it. There could be no other Motive, for, I am certain, there was no Mortal in the Universe more capable of leaving the proper Impressions of any Character whatever, on the Mind of those who were endowed with the necessary Talents to receive 'em.

I don't mention this with the least Tincture of Disregard to the dear Child, for I am well assured, she would have been glad to have rendered her Abilities useful to her unfortunate Aunt. And I dare say, *unless her Principles are perverted* (which, for her own sake, I hope are not,) she still retains in her Heart a secret Pity for my Sufferings! though to avow it might perhaps hazard the Forfeiture of that Blessing, Heaven has been pleased to make her Grandfather the happy Instrument of bestowing, which I would not for the Universe be the miserable Motive of, therefore shall not only excuse, but even advise her to think, *as some other of her Relations*

lations do, that I AM A STRANGER TO HER BLOOD.

'Tis plain the rancourous Hate to me had spread itself to so monstrous a Degree, that they rather chose to make themselves, I may say in this Case RIDICULOUSLY CRUEL, than not load me with an additional Weight of Misery. The low Malice of taking away the Child, as I had her Father's Consent, I put upon the Level of School-boys Understandings, who quarrel with their Playfellow, from a Jealousy of ones having more Plumbs in their Cake than t'others.

Had she staid, it might have been useful to both. As Time, Experience and Observation, had furnished me with some little Knowledge of the Stage, I would, to the Extent of my Power, have rendered it serviceable to my Niece; and, I am confident, she would, on her Part, by her Performance, have been greatly beneficial to me.

As I am foolishly flatter'd, from the Opinion of others, into a Belief of the Power of cultivating raw and unexperienced Geniuses, I design very shortly to endeavour to instruct those Persons who conceive themselves capable of dramatic Performances, and propose to make the Stage their Livelihood.

Some very good Friends of mine have lately advised me to this Scheme, which I shall put in Force as soon as I can with Conveniency, and will, on reasonable Terms, three Times a Week, pay constant Attendance from Ten in the Morning till Eight in the Evening, at my intended Academy. Where Ladies and Gentlemen shall be, to the utmost of my Power, instructed both in the Art of Speaking and Acting; that though they should never come upon the Stage, they shall be enabled even to read a Play more pleasingly to the Auditor, by a few necessary Hints, than 'tis likely they ever would without 'em.

If I should qualify those who may design to offer themselves to the Theatres, in such a Manner as may render them worthy the Managers Acceptance, I shall receive a double Satisfaction, both in regard to my Pupils Advancement, and rendering my academical Nursery useful to the Masters of both Houses, by a Cultivation of a good Genius; which has been often thrown away, like a Piece of fertile Ground over-run with Weeds, through Neglect or Want of good Husbandry.

When

When this Narrative is ended, I shall advertise to that Purpose in the daily Papers; and must now beg Leave to apologize for swelling out my Numbers with my own History, which was originally designed to have consisted only of a short Sketch of my *strange Life* But, on the Appearance of the first Number, I was enjoin'd (nay 'twas insisted on) by many, that if 'twas possible for me to enlarge the Account of myself to a Pocket Volume, I should do it.

In Compliance with so obliging a Request, which I receive as a Compliment from my good Friends, I have deferred the Publication of Mr. *Dumont*'s History 'till this is finish'd, which will be now in two *Saturdays* more; and I hope that, though the Town is not so well acquainted with the above-mention'd Gentleman, they will be equally curious to become so with his Story, as they have been with mine; and, I dare promise, that 'twill afford them such a Satisfaction in the reading, they won't repent their Encouragement of the Author

As Morality is the principal Foundation of the Work, I venture to recommend it to the Perusal of the Youthful of both Sexes, as

each

each will find a Character worthy their Observation, and, I hope, won't blush to make their Example

I intended to have made Writing my Support, if possible, when I was dispossessed of the Happiness of getting my Bread with my Brother, but my Cares increasing, I had not Time to settle myself properly, or collect my Mind for such an Undertaking, therefore was obliged to decline it, and trust to Providence from Time to Time for what I could get by occasionally Acting.

Though I was unfortunate in the Main, yet once in five or six Weeks something or other generally happened to relieve my afflicted Spirits, and I met with two Cards running that turn'd up Trumps, which led me into an imaginary Hope that the Measure of my Griefs were so compleatly filled, that 'twas they probable would contain no more.

The first of these unexpected Joys, arose from the tender Compassion of his late Grace the Duke of M-----gue, who, having been told of my hapless Fortune, gave so tender an Attention to it, it encouraged the Person who related it to advise me to write to his Grace.

I instantly

I instantly did, and, without the least Trouble of obtaining Admission for the Messenger or Letter, was relieved with several Guineas, enclosed in a Line of soft Commiseration, under the bounteous Hand of my noble Benefactor, the Honour of which, notwithstanding my Poverty, afforded me a more elevated Transport than the liberal Donation; and naturally claims a real Sorrow for his Loss, attended with a grateful and sincere Respect for his Memory, to the last Hour of my Existence, to which he has a Right from Hundreds more besides myself, having been a universal Physician, and Restorer of Peace and Comfort to afflicted Minds, variously oppressed.

This Comfort was, in about two Days, succeeded by an Engagement with the late (unfortunate) Mr *Russel*, who was then a Man of Vogue, and in universal Favour with every Person of Quality and Distinction. This Gentleman had an *Italian* Opera at Mr. *Hickford*'s Great Room, in *Brewer's-Street*, exhibited by Puppets; which I understanding the Management of, and the Language they sung, was hired, after the first Night's Performance, at a Guinea *per Diem*, to move his *Punch* in particular.

This

This Affair was carried on by Subscription, in as grand a Manner as possible. Ten of the best Hands in Town compleated his Band of Musick, and several of the Female Figures were ornamented with real Diamonds, lent for that Purpose by several Persons of the first Quality.

During the short Run I was, in respect of my Salary (which was paid me every Day of Performance) extreamly happy, but so unfortunately circumstanced, I was forced to set out between Five and Six o'Clock in the Morning, traversing St *James's-Park* 'till Mr *Hickford*'s Maid arose, and, for Security, staid there all Day, mingling with the thickest of the Croud at Night to get Home.

The Benefaction of my noble Friend, and Mr. *Russel*'s Salary, enabled me to new rig myself and Child; that is, upon the Score of Redemption. But this flowing Tide of Joy soon came to an Ebb, both with my Friend and Self, for, in a few Months after, I heard the unpleasing Tidings of his being under Confinement in *Newgate* for Debt.

Compassion led me to visit him there, though I had not Power to deliver him from
that

that dismal Abode, but in my Wishes: Though afterwards, had he taken my Advice, he might possibly have proved me a Friend by endeavouring to extricate him, in bringing on the *Hay-Market* Stage, a humourous Piece of his own Composing, which, I believe, is still in the Hands of some of his Creditors, where 'tis of no Use to the Person who possesses it, but, as it has Merit, might be rendered so, if properly disposed of.

I offered this unhappy Gentleman to provide Performers, with my own Service inclusive, and to take the entire Management of it upon myself, without Fee or Reward, unless his nightly Receipts empowered him to gratify me for my Trouble, which, had he but been barely set free, I should have thought myself amply rewarded, in being partly the happy Instrument.

As to the Money, I told him I would have nothing to do with it; that Door and Office-Keepers should be of his own providing, but that, if I engaged the People, they should be nightly paid, according to the Agreement I should make with them, and for myself, would, if the Thing succeeded, leave it to his Generosity to reward me as he thought proper, which I make no Doubt would have been

been done in the genteelest Manner, had the Affair been brought to any Issue

But this distressed Gentleman was madly exasperated with the terrible and sudden Revolution of his Fortune, and instead of receiving my offered Friendship with that Regard a reasonable Person might have thought it deserved, he rather seemed offended at the Proposal: Which startled me at first, but, on our farther Conversation, I was convinced of his growing Misfortune, and too plainly perceived that he was not entirely in his Senses, on which I dropped the Discourse, and, with a real Concern, left him that Evening, but returned to see him in about two Days, when instead of finding him in a more settled Order, he was absolutely changed from the Man of Sense to the driv'ling Ideot, nor was there the least Consistency in one single Syllable he uttered.

I found myself too much shocked to lengthen my Visit, and more so, when I gathered from him an Account, delivered with heart-breaking Sighs and bitter Sobs, that a Person he had entrusted to raise a Contribution for him among the Nobility, had run away with the Bounty intended for his Relief, and which would have more than effected it, as there
was

was upwards of an Hundred Pounds amassed for that Purpose.

This piteous Narration was recounted to me afterwards by a Gentleman, who was his intimate Friend, and had served him to the Extent of his Power through the whole Scene of Misery that ended him.

In about a Fortnight after my Interview with him in *Newgate*, passing through, I called to know how he did, and was informed he was removed by a *Habeas* to the *Fleet*. As it lay in my Way, I stopped there and enquired after him, upon which I was desired to walk up two Pair of Stairs, and in such a Room I should find him.

I expressed to the Persons who directed me a great Concern for him, and they as naturally answered, 'twas very kind and very good in me, and desired me very civilly to walk up, which accordingly I did, and, after having rambled into several Peoples Rooms through Mistake, I arrived at that where Mr *Russel*'s Remains only were deposited, for he was absolutely in a Coffin, which some Friend had sent in Respect to him

I conceive

I conceive a Description of my Surprize on this Account quite unnecessary, but I really, for some Time, was very near as motionless as the deceased Person, and in my Heart very angry with the Woman who sent me up to him, without informing me he was dead.

When I came down she very reasonably excused herself, by reminding me, that the Tenor of our Discourse consisted of nothing more than a tender Concern on my Side, for the unhappy Gentleman, and she concluded, that Friendship and Curiosity had brought me there to see his sad Remains, he having been dead two Days, and therefore she thought I knew it.

I assured her, I did not; and farther told her, I was pleased to see he had so handsome a Shroud and Coffin. But she shocked me excessively by telling me, he was to be removed out of the one and disrobed of the other, to be put into one provided by the Parish For 'twas a Law, when a Debtor died without any Effects or Means to satisfy their Creditors, they must be so interred, otherwise an Indulgence of being buried by Friends rendered the Warden of the *Fleet* liable to pay all the Debts of the Deceased, if it could be

proved

proved that he had suffered it -----'Tis a hard Case notwithstanding, that Humanity should not extend itself even to the Dead, without hurting those whose Principles of Christianity excite them to it.

Thus ended the Life of one who was universally admired, and had been for some Time as much the Fashion in Families as their Cloaths. But, alas! Misfortunes are too apt to wear out Friendship, and he was cast off in two or three Months with as much Contempt, as an old Coat made in *Oliver*'s Time.

Though it was represented to his Acquaintance, how cruelly he had been used by the Person he intrusted to follicit them in his Behalf, it was scarce believed, even by those who not long before had laid him nearest to their Hearts. This is one very remarkable Instance of the Uncertainty of Friendship, and the Instability of Peoples Minds who are only *fashionably kind*.

I was in Hopes, after Mr. *Ruffel*'s Death, to have got his Figures upon reasonable Terms, and have taken them into the Country, as they were very small, and rather an Incumbrance to one who did not understand how to make use of them; but, when I made an Enquiry into the Price of them, his Landlord valued them at Threescore Guineas, and the Money down.

That last Assertion soon ended my Project, as the Reader may conceive; so I engaged myself at *May-Fair*, and lived on my Profits there 'til the ensuing *Bartholomew*. From thence I went into the Country, where I remained ('till last *Christmas*) for very near nine Years.

My first Expedition was to *Sunning-Hill*, where I had the Joy of playing Capt *Flume*, and blending it with the Part of *Sylvia*. The Lady who should have represented it, as I suppose, was so strongly affected with the Death of her Brother *Owen*, she was not able to speak a plain Word, or indeed to keep her Ground.

This gave me an early Touch of the Quality of Strollers, and, but 'twas rather convenient than otherwise to keep out of Town, would soon have brought me back again. But, alas! this was trifling to what I afterwards beheld. I have seen an Emperor *as drunk as a Lord*, according to the old Phrase, and a Lord as elegant as a Ticket Porter. A Queen with one Ruffle on, and

Lord *Townly* without Shoes, or at least but an Apology for them.

This last Circumstance reminds me of the Queen in *The Spanish Fryar* once played without Stockings, though I must do the Person Justice to say, it proceeded from an unprecedented Instance of even a Superfluity of good Nature, which was excited by her Majesty's observing *Torrismond* to have a dirty Pair of Yarn Stockings, with above twenty Holes in Sight, and, as she thought her Legs not so much expos'd to View, kindly strips them of a fine Pair of Cotton, and lends them to the Hero.

I played *Lorenzo*, and, having no Business with the Queen, had a Mind to observe how she acquitted herself in her Part, being a Person I had known many Years, and was really anxious for her Success. I found she spoke sensibly, but, to my great Surprize, observed her to stoop extreamly forward, on which I concluded she was seized with a sudden Fit of the Cholick, but she satisfied me of the contrary, and, on her next Appearance, I remarked that she sunk down very much on that Side I stood between the Scenes, on which I then conjectured her to be troubled with a Sciatick Pain in her Side, and made a second Enquiry, but was answered in the Negative on that Score. Upon which I desired to know the Reason of her bending forward, and sideling so?

She told me, 'twas a Trick she had got. *'Tis a very new one then,* says I, *for I never knew you do so before*, but I began to suspect something was the Matter, and resolved to find it out. Presently the Royal Dame was obliged to descend from the Stage into the Dressing-Room, and made a Discovery, by the tossing up of her Hoop, of a Pair of naked Legs.

I own, I was both angry and pleased. I was concerned to find my Friend's Humanity had extended so far as to render herself ridiculous, besides the Hazard she run of catching Cold. But must confess, I never saw so strong a Proof of good Nature, especially among Travelling-Tragedizers; for, to speak Truth of them, they have but a small Share of that Principle subsisting amongst them.

If a Person is but a lame Hand, he or she is despised for that; and, 'tis a common Rule, when Benefits come on, to say among their different Parties (which they all herd in) Mr and Mrs. *Such a-one*, to be sure, will have a
great

great House, meaning perhaps the Manager and his Wife, who very often are the worst in the whole Set. And 'tis very seldom that one Couple shall both prove good, but the Merit of the one is forced to make up for the Deficiency of the other.

The least Glimmering or Shade of Acting, in Man or Woman, is a sure Motive of Envy in the rest; and, if their Malice can't perswade the Town's-People into a Dislike of their Performance, they'll cruelly endeavour to taint their Characters; so that I think going a Strolling is engaging in a little, dirty Kind of War, in which I have been obliged to fight so many Battles, I have resolutely determined to throw down my Commission. And to say Truth, I am not only sick, but heartily ashamed of it, as I have had nine Years Experience of its being a very contemptible Life; rendred so, through the impudent and ignorant Behaviour of the Generality of those who pursue it; and I think it wou'd be more reputable to earn a Groat a Day in Cinder-sifting at *Tottenham-Court*, than to be concerned with them.

'Tis a Pity that so many, who have good Trades, should idly quit them, to become despicable Actors, which renders them

Q 3 useless

useless to themselves, and very often Nusances to others. Those who were bred up in the Profession, have the best Right to make it their Calling; but their Rights are horribly invaded by Barbers 'Prentices, Taylors and Journeymen Weavers, all which bear such strong Marks of their Professions, that I have seen *Richard* the Third murder *Henry* the Sixth with a Shuttle, and *Orestes* jump off the Shop-Board to address *Hermione*

Another Set of Gentry who have crept into their Community, are Servants out of Place, and I very lately saw the gallant *Marcian*, as well rubbed and curried, as ever the Actor did a Horse in his Master's Stable. This worthy Wight having the Happiness to write an exceeding fine Hand, and living formerly with a Gentleman in one of the Inns of Court, wisely palms himself upon Strangers for a Lawyer, when his real and original Profession was that of a Groom.

How such Sort of People, without the Help of at least a little Education, can presume to pick the Pockets of an Audience, is to me astonishing, though they have the Vanity and Assurance to say they please, but 'tis only themselves, and were the Spirits of departed Poets to see their Works mangled and butchered,

butchered, as I have too often been a melancholly Witness of, they would certainly kick the depredating Heroes out of this World into the next.

I have had the Mortification of hearing the Characters of *Hamlet*, *Varanes*, *Othello*, and many more Capitals, rent in Pieces by a Figure no higher than two Six-penny Loaves, and a Diſſonancy of Voice, which conveyed to me a ſtrong Idea of a Cat in Labour, all which, conjoined with an injudicious Utterance, made up a compleat tragical Emetick, for a Perſon of the ſmalleſt Degree of Judgment. And yet theſe Wretches very impudently ſtile themſelves Players, a Name, let me tell them, when properly applied, is an Honour to an Underſtanding, for none can deſerve that Title, who labour under the Want of a very conſiderable Share of Senſe.

In the Courſe of my Travels, I went to a Town called *Cirenceſter*, in *Glouceſterſhire*, when an odd Affair happened, which I beg Leave to relate, as follows.

I happened to be taken violently ill with a nervous Fever and Lowneſs of Spirits, that continued upon me for upwards of three Years, before I was able to get the better of it

When

When I came to the before-mentioned Town, I was so near Death, that my Dissolution was every Moment expected; but, after my Illness came to a Crisis, I very slowly amended, and as soon as I could creep about the House was advised, by my Apothecary, to ride out, if I was able to sit a Horse

As soon as I found myself capable of it, I followed his Advice, and had one lent me for myself, and another for my Friend, the good-natured Gentlewoman who commiserated poor *Torrismond*'s Misfortune, and to whom I am most infinitely and sincerely obliged for her tender Care in nursing me in three Years Illness, without repining at her Fatigue, which was uninterrupted, and naturally fixes on me a lasting grateful Sense of the Favour.

The Person who furnished me with the Horses, was a reverend-looking Elder, about sixty Years of Age, with a beautiful curling Head of Hair and florid Complexion, that bespoke at once both Admiration and Respect His Temper was agreeable to his Aspect, extreamly pleasing, and his Company entertaining, with which he often obliged me, while my Friend attended her Business of a Play Night.

After

After riding out two or three Days, the old Gentleman perceiving me to grow better, asked me, if I liked the Horse? which I told him I greatly approved, as it was an easy and willing Creature. He said, he was at my Service. I very thankfully accepted the Favour, and, before many Witnesses, the Present was made; as also the other for my Friend's Use, which belonged to a young Fellow he called his Nephew.

He told me, that if I thought proper to quit the Stage, which he imagined, in my weak Condition, was better avoided than pursued, he would take me to his Estate, situate at a Place called *Brill*, in *Oxfordshire*, and, if I and my Friend would stay with him as long as either he or we should live, I should be Superintendant over his Affairs Abroad, and my Friend should have the entire Management of the Family at Home, which, he said, consisted only of himself and Nephew, and about seven or eight Servants, that were employed in Husbandry, he being, as he informed us, a wealthy Grazier.

'Twas soon resolved, that we should give Warning to Mr *Linnett*, who was Manager of the Company, to leave him at the Expiration of of a Month. This was accordingly done, and, as a Confirmation of his Intention in taking us with him, gave Mrs *Brown* an old-fashioned Gold Necklace, with a large Locket of the same Metal, which altogether, I dare believe by the Weight, could not be worth less than Twenty Pounds, there being several Rows, and the Beads not small.

I desired the old Gentleman not to insist on her wearing it, 'till she went Home. It being an old-fashioned Thing I knew, as an Actress, People would stare to see her so equipped, though it was a valuable Gift, but more proper to ornament the Neck of a Country-Housewife, than a Tragedy-Queen. I therefore desired him to keep it, 'till we were settled, and pretended, for fear of affronting him, that she might run a Hazard in losing it of a Play-Night. He thought my Care was just, but insisted on her laying it up herself, and I luckily insisted he should have it in his Possession 'till we went away.

The Thoughts of being so well settled and provided for both our Lives, was, in Fact, greatly conducive towards the Restoration of my Health, and our Friendship with the old Gentleman daily encreased, as also with his Nephew, whom he frequently sent into our

ferent Parts of the Country after Cattle, and, with the utmost Ceremony, begged the Favour of borrowing my Horse, 'till he could send an Order to *Brill* for another.

The least I could do was to comply with the Request of so valuable a Friend, and away went the Nephew; who, at length, happened to stay three or four Days longer than was intended, which gave his Uncle a great deal of seeming Uneasiness, that, to all Appearance, was worked into a downright Passion, with Threats of cutting him of with a Shilling, for rambling about when he had sent him upon Business of weighty Concern.

As I observed him to be very much out of Humour, I thought it would be but a friendly Part to endeavour to appease the Uncle, for the Nephew's sake, which the old Man took very kindly of me, and bid me want for nothing that might be necessary towards the Recovery of my Health, assuring me, when *Jemmy* came Home, Fifty Pounds should be at my Service, to put to what Use I pleased

So generous an Offer, unasked, made me conceive that this Man was dropped from Heaven, to be my kind Deliverer from all the

Sorrows

Sorrows of Life, but, before Mr. *James* came back, there came a sudden Order from the Magistrate of the Town, to insist on the old Man's leaving it at a Moment's Warning, on Pain of being sent to *Gloucester* Jail, if he refused to obey.

In the Interim, Home comes the Nephew, who received the same Charge, but they huddled up their Affairs in a strange Manner, and ventured to stay three Days longer, though very little seen.

This put my Friend and self into a terrible Consternation, for still we could neither of us arrive at the real Truth of the Affair, 'till Mr. *Linnett*, who had heard it from the Town's-People, and, with a frighted Aspect and real Concern, came almost breathless to let me know, that my pretended Friends were positively Gamblers and House-breakers; that if we listened any longer to them, we should be sure not only to be deceived, but, in all human Probability, be made innocent Sufferers for their Guilt.

Mr *Linnett*'s Concern was expressed with all the Symptoms of strong Truth, which startled us both with Fear and Wonder, and made us heedfully attentive to all he related.

We

We immediately gave up all Right and Claim to our Horses, and my Friend did the same to her Gold Necklace, all which were stolen Goods, and, had she been seen with it about her Neck by the right Owner, 'tis possible the poor Soul might have been provided with one of a rougher Kind, and each of us disgracefully exalted, for being harmlessly credulous.

I afterwards found out, their Scheme was to have got our Boxes into their Possession, which, as both the old and young Man were frequent in their Visits to play at Cards with me, by Way of Amusement in my Illness, they had observed were well furnished with very good Linnen, and my Friend had just received a Present of Cloaths from her Relations. Had they got these into their Possession, they would have proved a tolerable Booty

But our better Stars shone forth that Time, and though we lost only an imaginary Fortune, we secured our Lives, and the little All we were both worth upon the Face of the Earth.

In about a Year after, the old Man dangled into the next World upon a Gibbet, either

ther at *Salisbury* or *Oxford*, which I cannot positively affirm, but that was his deserved Fate, and the young one died raving mad in a Prison, in or near *London*.

I thought proper to insert this Story, not only as it is a particular Occurrence of my Life, but to warn the undesigning Part of the World of heedlessly falling into Company of Strangers, and being taken in by them.

This Man, by his Discourse and Appearance, would have deceived a much wiser Person than myself, as he really wore the venerable Marks of bearded Sanctity and Wisdom, but his Principles were as opposite to that Description, as an Angel to a Dæmon, having been upwards of forty Years a noted Gambler, Pickpocket, and sometimes Highwayman.

I often lift up my Heart to Heaven, with grateful Sense of its providential Care of us, in preventing the dismal Scenes of Misery to which we should have been exposed, had this wicked Man perpetrated his Design, and we might have been made innocent Sacrifices to save his horrid Life, through Villainy imposed, and branded with the Guilt of Crimes we never should have thought of committing

I therefore

I therefore hope, our fortunate Escape will set others on their Guard, who may be liable to an Accident of the same Kind.

When we left *Cirencester*, we made a short Progress to *Chippenham*, an agreeably situated Market-Town in the Road to *Bath*, where I met with many Friends, as indeed I generally had the good Fortune to do, go where I would, in particular Mr *Thomas Stroud*, who keeps the *Angel* Inn, and Mr *Lodge*, Master of the *White Hart*, were conjunctive in forwarding my Interest. And I think, without Compliment to either, they are remarkable for keeping two of the most elegant and best accommodated Houses throughout *Great-Britain*. A Thing seldom known, that one little Market-Town should produce two such agreeable Repositories for Travellers, and I am very glad they meet with the Success they deservedly enjoy.

From thence we took a short Trip to a little Village called *Corsham*, four Miles distant from *Chippenham*, where we had little else to do than to walk out and furnish our keen Stomachs with fresh Air, and come Home and gape at each other for want of a Dinner.

Bad Business is a sure Means to produce ill Blood in a Company, for, as they grow hungry, they naturally grow peevish, and fall out with one another, without considering that each bears a proportionable Part of the Distress, the Manager excepted, who never fails, in all Companies, to eat, as *Bombardinian* says,

"*Tho' all Mankind shou'd starve.*"

This happening to be my Case, I was refused a small, but needful Supply, which occasioned a disagreeable Argument; and I wrote to Mr *Richard Elrington* to inform him, agreeable to an Invitation I received some Months before, upon his sending me three Guineas, my Friend, Daughter, and Self, would immediately join him.

Accordingly as soon as the Letter could reach him, which was as far as *Tiverton* in *Devonshire*, he dispatched a Messenger on Horseback, with two Guineas and an Half, and a Letter full of Joy with the Hopes of my speedy Arrival, which was no small Advantage, as the Company then stood, as it consisted but of few Hands, and one of the Women so-unfortunate, that she was dead drunk

drunk in Bed the first Night of their Opening, when she should have been soberly employed in the Performance of *Lucy* in *The Beggar's Opera*. Mrs *Elrington*, who was perfect in all the Characters in that Piece, artfully contrived to double the Parts of *Polly* and *Lucy*; which, I suppose, she must do, as *Sosia* represents himself and *Alcmena*, by the Assistance of a Lanthorn.

So dismal a Disappointment naturally offended the Audience, and their nightly Receipts fell very short of their Expectations from this disastrous Chance, which reduced them to the Necessity of playing three Times a Week at a little Market-Town, called *Columpton*, within five Miles of *Tiverton*, or at least attempting so to do, that they might have a Probability of eating once in six Days; and a terrible Hazard that was, for the *Columpton* Audience never amounted to more than Twenty Shillings at the fullest House, which, when the Charges were paid, and the Players like so many hungry Magpies, had gaped for their Profits, might very possibly afford what they call a Stock-Supper, which was generally ended in a Quarrel, by Way of Desert.

That barbarous Word MERIT, has been the Occasion of more Fewds in those Communities than the whole Court of *Chancery* can ever be able to decide, or His Majesty's Army overcome. I own it surprizes me that a single Syllable, which in itself is truly valuable, should be so constant an Invader of the Peace of those, who, if I may judge by their Abuse of it on the Stage, are perfect Strangers to its Derivation, and not in the least relative to them who nightly claim an unlawful Title to it.

However I shall, though I find Fault with the Multitude, do Justice to those who deserve it. Mrs *Elrington* has the first Demand on my Judgment in that Case, among the Travelling-Comedians. She has a great deal of Spirit, and speaks sensibly. Her Genius is calculated for Low-Comedy entirely, and the Smallness of her Person, which rendred her unsuccessful in her Attempt on *Covent Garden* Theatre, is no Detriment on a Country Stage, as the Difference of them is upon an Equality with a Mouse-trap and a Mountain.

When we arrived at *Tiverton*, they were gone for a Night or two to their more Rural Retreat,

Retreat; and I having a Man and two Horses to discharge, was really, with our Keeping upon the Road for near seventy Miles, under some Sort of Confusion and Concern, for want of the Half Guinea which was short of our Demands.

After some private Consultation with my Friend and Daughter, who were both trembling with terrible Apprehensions of some Immunities arising from this Misfortune, I took Heart, and resolved to set the best Face upon a bad Matter. As Mr *Elrington* was not present to receive us, I enquired what Houses he used in Town, and was, to my great Joy, soon informed that there was one in particular, the Mistress of which was a great Friend to him, on which I undauntedly set forward, and very luckily found the Person to be the young Man's Mother who brought us the Money into *Wiltshire*.

In Mr. *Elrington*'s Name I borrowed the Half Guinea, which, to our general Joy, was immediately granted, and the Man and Horses discharged, though a second Thought came into my Head, that as the Company was absent, and hearing but a terrible Account of their Progress there, I began to be doubtful whether their Faith was strong enough to keep

keep so many poor, pennyless Devils from starving, 'till their Return, which I was told would not be so soon as they proposed, there being a Play bespoke, to which they were promised a great House.

This gave me fresh Spirits, and I thought it quite proper to engage our Guide to walk the other five Miles and escort us to the Players. The Splendour of a Shilling soon prevailed, and we mounted directly, my Friend single, and my Daughter and Self double, upon a strapping Beast, which was of a proper Size to have been rank'd in the Number of Dragoons.

I was not a little pleased, notwithstanding their ill Success, to find Mr. *Elrington*'s Credit so good, and his Character so justifiable, that, even in his Absence, a Stranger could be intrusted on his Account.

When we came to our Journey's End, Mrs. *Elrington*, who was the first Person we saw, received us with inexpressible Joy, and gave us a second Relation of the miserable State of their Affairs: But, as Lady *Grace* says of Lady *Townly*, *She rallied her Misfortunes with such Vivacity*, that had not her Wit been *too strong* for my Resolution, I should have

have certainly gone back again *by the Return of the next Post.*

As we were just entring the Town, a goodlooking Farmer met us, by our Appearance guess'd what we were, and ask'd if we were not Comedians? We answered in the Affirmative, on which he desired, if we had any Pity for ourselves, to turn back, and, rapping out a thundring Oath, affirmed to us that we were going to starve, which threw my Friend (who is not the best Horsewoman in the World) into such a Fright, she dropp'd her Bridle, from which Advantage her hungry Steed fairly run her into a Hedge, and dropp'd her into the Ditch.

When she recovered her Surprize, she was for going directly back, without seeing the Company; but when I assured her the Money would not hold out, she was prevailed on to go forward.

At length the bespoke Play was to be enacted, which was *The Beaux Stratagem*, but such an Audience, I dare believe, was never heard of before or since. In the first Row of the Pit sat a Range of drunken Butchers, some of whom soon entertained us with the inharmonious Musick of their Nostrils

Nostrils. Behind them were seated, as I suppose, their unsizable Consorts, who seemed to enjoy the same State of Happiness their dear Spouses were possessed of, but, having more Vivacity than the Males, laugh'd " *and* " *talk'd louder than the Players.*"

Mrs. *Elrington* (who play'd Mrs *Sullen*) having such a lovely Prospect before her, and being willing to divert me from any Design she might suspect of my not staying, in the drunken Scene between *Archer* and *Scrub* (the former of which I play'd) unexpectedly paid us a Visit, and, taking the Tankard out of *Scrub*'s Hand, drank Mr *Archer*'s Health, and to our better Acquaintance. The least I could do was to return the Lady's Compliment, by drinking to her's, after which she ordered my Brother *Scrub* to call the Butler in with his Fiddle, and insisted on my dancing a Minuet with her, while poor *Scrub* comforted himself with the Remains of the Tankard.

This Absurdity led us into several more, for we both took a Wild-goose Chace through all the dramatic Authors we could recollect, taking particular Care not to let any single Speech bear in the Answer the least Affinity, and, while I was making Love from *Jaffier*,

she

she tenderly approved my Passion with the Soliloquy of *Cato*.

In this incoherent Manner we finished the Night's Entertainment. Mrs. *Sullen*, instead of *Archer*, concluding the Play with *Jane Shore*'s Tag, at the End of the first Act of that Tragedy, to the universal Satisfaction of that Part of the Audience who were awake, and were the reeling Conductors of those, who only *dreamt* of what they should have *seen*.

For some Time we drag'd on our unsuccessful Lives, without the least Prospect of an Alteration, that I at last gave up all Hopes and Expectations of ever enjoying a happy Moment. This, according to the usual Custom, made each wear an Eye of Coldness and Dislike, 'till, after a long Series of Plagues, Madam *Fortune*, in one of her Frolicks, was pleased to pay us a small Visit, and during her short Stay we began to be better reconciled, 'till the trumpery Slut tucked up her Tail of good Nature, and reduced us to our primitive Nothing, and sour Looks, with disaffected Minds, resumed their Empire in the Breast of every Malecontent

In

In Process of Time we went to *Cirencester*, where I informed the Reader I had been once before, with Mr *Linnett*'s Company. But Mr *Elrington*, without any previous Notice, took a Place in the Stage-Coach for *London*, and, the very Night we came to the Town, left his Wife to manage the Company; in which I gave my Assistance, to take off from her as much of the Trouble as I possibly could.

Mr. *Linnett*, wanting at that Time some Auxiliaries, sent one of his Company to engage me and my Friend to join him at *Bath*, where he then was, in a new-erected Theatre in *Kingsmead-Street*. But my Honour was so deeply engaged in Mrs. *Elrington*'s Behalf, I would, on no Terms, leave her, as she was pleased to compliment me with being her Right-hand; and, at that Time, not knowing the real Design of her Husband's going to *London*, looked on her as an injured Person, which doubly engaged my Attachment to her Interest. Though, I afterwards found, it was a concerted Scheme to fix himself, if possible, with Mr. *Rich*, which proved almost abortive, he staying but one Season, from what Cause I shan't pretend to judge, and then went to *Bath*.

His Wife soon followed, and I was left with six more besides myself. One Scene and a Curtain, with some of the worst of their Wardrobe, made up the *Paraphanalia* of the Stage, of which I was Prime Minister; and, though under as many Disadvantages as a Set of miserable Mortals could patiently endure, from the before-mentioned Reasons, and an inexhaustible Fund of Poverty, through the General Bank of the whole Company, even to a Necessity of borrowing Morey to pay the Carriage to the next Town, we all went into a joint Resolution to be industrious; and got a Sufficiency to support ourselves and pay the Way, not only to that Town, but were decently set down in the next, with just enough to dismiss our Waggoner with Reputation, and were then left to proceed upon fresh Credit, and contract the strongest Friendship we could with each believing Landlord.

As 'tis very common for even the lowest in Understanding to fancy themselves Judges of Acting, I must give a curious Specimen of it in a Person who saw me, for want of a better, attempt the Part of *Hamlet.*

Hamlet. I was lucky enough to gain a Place in his Opinion; and he was pleased to express his Approbation of me, by saying no Man could possibly do it better, because *I so frequently broke out in fresh Places*.

But I had a much larger Share of his Esteem after playing *Scrub*, which was indeed infinitely more suitable to his Taste, and left so strong an Impression on his Mind, that a Night or two after, when I was tragedizing in the Part of *Pyrrhus*, in *The Distress'd Mother*, he stepped from the Pit, and desired me to oblige some of his Friends, as well as himself, by mixing a few of *Scrub*'s Speeches in the Play, assuring me, it would give much more Satisfaction to the Spectators, though they liked me very well, he said, in the Part I was acting.

This revived in my Memory the curious Performance at *Columpton*, and rendred me, for the rest of the Night, infinitely a properer Person for *Scrub* than *Pyrrhus*, as the Strangeness of his Fancy had such an Effect on my risible Faculties, I thought I should never close my Mouth again in the least Degree of Seriosity.

I imagine

I imagine it is such Judges as these, that occasion that indolent Stupefaction in most Travelling-Players, and, as the lower Sort are foolish enough to be pleased with Buffoonery in Comedy, and Bellowing in Tragedy, without a Regard to Sense or Nature in either, it makes them forgetful that there are, among the Country Gentlemen and Ladies, very great Judges, whose good Nature over-looks those monstrous Absurdities, but, at the same Time, if they took more Pains to please them, they would certainly find them more frequent in their Visitation

It is for want of this Consideration in the Players, which makes the Favours they receive from Families of Distinction rather a Charity, than a genteel Reward, for, at best, their weak Endeavours to entertain a Set of sensible People, who would be glad to encourage the least Spark of Decency and Industry.

I know this will be a Kind of Choak-pear to many of the Travelling-Gentry, but I am under no Sort of Uneasiness on that Account; and think, if they make a proper Use of the Hint,

Hint, they will have more Reason to thank me, than be offended at it.

After traversing through some few Towns more, Mr. and Mrs *Elrington* rejoin'd their Company, and we went to a Place called *Minchin-Hampton*, in *Gloucestershire*, where we were kindly invited by the Lord of the Manor, a worthy Gentleman; who was not only a great Benefactor, in Respect of the Business, but our Guardian and Protector, from the terrible Consequences that might have ensued from a most shocking Cruelty, designed for the Company in general; but, luckily for the rest, only put in Force against me and two more. Which was, by Dint of an Information, encouraged by a C-----r at S-----d who meanly supported a decayed Relation, by procuring him a special Warrant to apprehend all Persons within the Limits of the Act of Parliament.

This ignorant Blockhead carried his Authority beyond a legal Power, for almost every Traveller that went through the Town was examined by him, before they could pass freely, and often made Sacrifices to his Interest.

My

My Landlord, who was a worthy Wight likewise, was privy to the Plot laid against us; though affected infinite Concern when we were taken, and violently exclaimed against his Partner in this Contrivance, tho' they were equally concern'd. The Scheme was not intended to do Justice in regard to the Laws, but extort Money from the Players and the worthy Gentlemen, who, they were well assured, would stand by us in a Case of Extremity, as indeed he did. They carried on their Process so far, as to take me and two of our Men, to Jail, where we were not under the least Apprehensions of going, from what my Landlord had told us.

We waited in Court, expecting every Moment to be called upon, and dismissed with a slight Reprimand: But, alas! 'twas not so easy as we thought, for we were beckoned to the other End of the Court, and told, that the Keeper of the Prison insisted on our going into the Jail, only for a Shew, and to say we had been under Lock and Key. An Honour, I confess, I was not in the least ambitious of, and for the Show, I thought 'twould never be over, for it lasted from Nine in the Morning 'till the same Hour of the next, and had it not been for the generous and friendly Assistance of the before-mention'd Gentleman, I believe it would have held out 'till *Doom's-day* with me, for another Day must have absolutely put an End to my Life.

Rage and Indignation having wrought such an Effect on my Mind, it threw me almost into a Frenzy, and arose to such a Height, that I very cordially desired my Fellow-Prisoners would give me Leave to cut their Throats, with a faithful Promise to do the same by my own, in Case we were doomed to remain there after the Tryal.

They were sorry to see me, they said, so very much disconcerted, but could by no Means comply with my Request, endeavouring, as much as possible, to keep up my Spirits, and bring me into Temper.

Several Times my Landlord came Backwards and Forwards, giving us false Hopes of our being every Minute called upon. The last Visit he made, I began to be quite outragious,

outragious, and told him all I conceived of him, uttering several bold Truths, not in the least to the Advantage of his Character.

Away he went grumbling, and I never saw him 'till the next Morning, when he came to summons us to the Hall. The Evening wore apace, and the Clock struck Eight, the dreadful Signal for the Gates to be lock'd up for the Night.

I offered Half a Guinea apiece for Beds, but was denied them; and, if I had not fortunately been acquainted with the Turnkey, who was a very good-natured Fellow, we must have been turn'd into a Place to lie upon the bare Ground, and have mixed among the Felons, whose Chains were rattling all Night long, and made the most hideous Noise I ever heard, there being upwards of two hundred Men and Boys under the different Sentences of Death and Transportation.

Their Rags and Misery gave me so shocking an Idea, I begged the Man, in Pity, to hang us all three, rather than put us among such a dreadful Crew. The very Stench of them,

them, would have been a sufficient Remedy against any future Ills that could have happened to me; but those dreadful Apprehensions were soon ended, by the young Fellow who was our Wardour for the Night, making Interest with a Couple of Shoe-Makers, who were imprisoned in the Womens Condemn'd-Hole, which, till they came, had not been occupied for a considerable Time.

These two Persons were confined, one for Debt, the other for having left his Family, with a Design to impose his Wife and Children on the Parish.

Extreamly glad were we to be admitted into the dismal Cell; which, though the Walls and Flooring were formed of Flint, at that Time I was proud of entering, as the Men were neat, and their Bed (which my Companions only took Part of) entirely clean.

The two Gentlemen of the Craft had, the Day we were brought in, furnished themselves with each a Skin, for Under-Leathers, which, being hollow, one within the other, I chose for my Dormitory, and having a Pair of Boots on and a Great Coat,

Coat, rolled into my Leathern Couch, secure from every Evil that might occur from such a Place, except a Cold which I got, occasioned by the Dampness of my Bed-chamber.

As we were not there for any Crime, *but that committed by those who informed against us*, I had the good Fortune to prevail on my Friend the Turnkey to permit me to send for Candles and some good Liquor, to reward our kind Hosts, and preserve us from the dreadful Apprehensions of getting each an Ague in our petrified Apartment.

I continued, for the most Part of the Night, very low spirited and in very ill Humour, 'till I was roused by the Drollery of one Mr *Maxfield*, my Fellow-Sufferer, a good-natured Man, and of an odd Turn of Humour, who would not let me indulge my Melancholly, which he saw had strongly possessed me, and insisted, as he had often seen me exhibit Captain *Macheath* in a Sham-Prison, I should, as I was then actually in the Condemned-Hold, sing all the Bead-roll of Songs in the last Act, that he might have the Pleasure of saying,

saying, I had once performed IN CHA-
RACTER.

I own, I was not in a Condition to be chearful, but the tender Concern of those about me laid a Kind of Constraint on me to throw off my Chagrin, and comply with their Request; which, when ended, I fairly fell asleep for about an Hour, and dreamt of all the Plagues that had tormented my Spirits in the Day.

As soon as the Dawn of Day appeared, I sat with impatient Expectation of the Turnkey's coming to let me into the fresh Air, and, to do him Justice, he came an Hour earlier on my Account to let us all look into the Yard, which is formed into Gravel-Walks, not unlike *Gray's-Inn* Gardens, though not kept up in that regular and nice Order.

But rough as it was, I thought it comparable to the Garden of *Eden*, and question much, when the first Pair beheld their Paradise, whether they were more transported at the View, than I was when let out of my Cell

After

After I had sauntered about for a Quarter of an Hour, deeply immersed in Thought, down came the rattling Crew, whose hedious Forms and dreadful Aspects, gave me an Idea of such Horrors, which can only be supposed to centre in Hell itself. Each had his Crime strongly imprinted on his Visage, without the least Tincture of Remorse or Shame; and, instead of imploring for Mercy, impudently and blasphemously arraigned the Judgment of the Power Divine, in bringing them to the Seat of Justice.

While I was surveying these miserable and dreadful Objects, I could not possibly refrain from Tears, to see so many of my Fellow-Creatures entered Volunteers in the Service of that Being which is hourly preying upon the weak and negligent Part of Mankind; and, as I too plainly saw, both Age and Infancy plunged in total, undistinguished Ruin.

About the Hour of Eight, we received the pleasing News of our being ordered to appear in Court at Nine; and, the Joy of being removed, though but for a few Moments, from the Sight of these unhappy Wretches, was
superior

superior to that I felt, when delivered from the torturing Apprehension I had some Years before of ending my Life, by Famine, in the *Marshalsea*.

But then the Dread of being remanded back to Prison suddenly gave a Damp to my Transport; but, Heaven be praised, our kind Benefactor sent in the Night a special Messenger to be ready in the Sessions-House, with a large Quantity of Gold, to protect us from any threatning Danger.

I had not been in the Pen five Minutes, before I was call'd upon to receive a Letter of Comfort to myself and Friends; who, tho' they assumed a Gaiety the Night before, were heartily shock'd at appearing at the Bar among a Set of Criminals, the least of whose Crimes not one of them would have dared to have been guilty of, though but in Thought.

However, we had the Pleasure to see the wise J----- (who, for Dint of Interest to his Kinsman, committed us) march out of Court just before our Cause came on, which ended in a very few Words, our kind Protector having laid our Plan of Safety so securely with his Interest and Power, we were soon dismissed;

missed; and can never, I think, be sufficiently grateful in our Acknowledgements, for so tender and generous a Commiseration of our Misfortune.

'Twas a secret Pleasure to us, to know that the C-----r was obliged to walk off, having rendred himself so contemptible to the Gentlemen on the Bench, by dabbling in such dirty Work, that he was not only heartily despised by them, but stood a ridiculous Chance, if he had staid 'till our Dismission, of being hooted out of Court. And, I believe, if he were to live to the Age of *Methuselah*, this great Action of his Life would not be forgot.

'Tis no small Comfort to me, that some of the best Gentlemen in and about that Place have dropped his Acquaintance on the Account, as they conceived a Man of Sense might have employed his Time and Thoughts more laudably, than in giving Countenance and Encouragement to an Action, which was founded upon Avarice, not Justice. For I can be upon Oath, and bring many more to justify the Truth of my Assertion, that they brought in a Bill of different Charges to the Amount of near Twelve Pounds, besides a Quantity of Guineas it cost the Gentleman who stood our Friend in the Affair.

have

I have often heard of Peoples paying Money to avoid a Jail, but we were so cruelly imposed on, they made us pay Half a Guinea a-piece for going into one, and, though we had but twelve Post-Miles to ride, charged a Guinea a Head for conducting us to G------, besides the Expences of our Horses, which they ought to have found us, as we were afterwards informed.

Power, when invested in the Hands of Knaves or Fools, generally is the Source of Tyranny, which has been too often experienced. And had not our worthy Friend stood firmly by us, we must have innocently suffered, for labouring to keep ourselves just above the Fears of starving.

As we were not guilty of any Misdemeanor every Body pitied our Distress, and heartily despised the Author of it. Our Friend, who gave us partly an Invitation, as he was a Person of great Worth and Power, was highly exasperated, and took it as a high Indignity offered to himself, after he had given us Encouragement to presume to object against his entertaining his Family (which was a numerous one) in an inoffensive Manner, and which, as he reasonably urged, kept many an

idle

idle Person from lavishing their Substance at Alehouses, equally destructive to their Healths and the Interest of their Wives and Children.

On our Return from G----, the Gentleman bespoke a Play, and removed us out of the Little Town-Hall into the Great One, which was his Property, and, in despight of our Adversaries, supported us, with a firm Promise to protect us, in Case of a second Invasion, if it cost him Half his Estate. But, as they knew his Power and Resolution both invincible, they never attempted to molest us afterwards.

Our Stay was but short, after this unlucky Stroke of Fortune, though it was a bad Matter well ended, Thanks to the Humanity of our generous Friend. We were heartily glad when we left the Place; and whenever I go to that, or any other, upon the same Expedition, I'll give them leave to imprison me for every Hour of Life to come.

The Autumn following Mr *Elrington* and his Spouse went again to *Bath*, and I was left as Conductor to the Company a second Time. Just before they went, a Plot was laid to draw us into another Dilemma at *Dursley*; but we were upon our Guard, and luckily escaped

escaped their Persecution. In order to get quite out of their Reach, we went into another County, to a Town called *Rofs* in *Herefordshire*, where we met with tolerable Success, and from thence proceeded to *Monmouth*, in *Wales*; which, though a very large Place, we found it very difficult to get a bare Livelihood.

Chepstow was our next Station, where I met with many Friends, particularly a Widow Lady, to whom, and her Family in general, I am under great Obligations, and shall ever with Pride acknowledge.

I had the Honour and Happiness of obtaining the Friendship of another Lady, who lived within a Quarter of a Mile of *Chepstow*, and often favoured me with friendly Letters when I went to *Abergavenny*; at the End of which Town I left Mr. *Elrington*, with a firm Design, at that Time, to quit all Thoughts of Playing.

I immediately took a very handsome House with a large Garden, consisting of near three Quarters of an Acre of Ground, belonging to my Friend's Papa, a very worthy Gentleman, who had eminently distinguished himself in Battle, in the Reigns of King *William* and Queen

Queen *Anne*, but, in the Decline of Life, quitted the Service, and retired, having a very considerable Estate, to which his Daughter is sole Heiress.

Perhaps the Reader may think, that the repeated Rebuffs of Fortune might have brought me to some Degree of Reflection, which might have regulated the Actions of my Life; but, that I may not impose upon the Opinions of the good-natured Part of the World, who might charitably bestow a favourable Thought on me in that Point, I must inform them, that the Aversion I had conceived for Vagabondizing (for such I shall ever esteem it) and the good Nature of my Friends in *Chepstow*, put it strongly in my Head to settle there, to which End I determined to turn Pastry-Cook and Farmer, and, without a Shilling in the Universe, or really a positive Knowledge where to get one, took Horse from *Abergavenny* to visit the young Lady, and hire the House.

I must do her the Justice to say she advised me to forgoe my Resolution, and set before me all the Inconveniencies I afterwards laboured under. But she found me so determined, she dropped her Argument; and, being of an obliging Temper, forwarded the repairing of the House, that it might be ready,

ready, at the appointed Time, for my Reception.

To be short, I went to it, but, that the whole Scene of my unaccountable Farce might be compleat, I not only involved myself, but the Gentlewoman, whom I have before-mentioned, that travelled with me, in the same needless and unreasonable Difficulties, for which I think myself bound in Honour to ask her Pardon, as I really was the Author of many Troubles, from my inconsiderate Folly, which nothing but a sincere Friendship, and an uncommon Easiness of Temper, could have inspired her either to have brooked or to have forgiven.

As soon as I arrived at *Chepstow* I began to consider, that though I had got a House without either Bed or Chair to lie or sit on, it would be highly proper to seek out a Place of Rest, and, that I might live as cheap as possible, took a ready-furnished Lodging for Nights, and wandered for a Fortnight up and down my empty House, 'till Fortune came that Road to drop some Furniture into it.

I own it, I was secretly chagrin'd at my Exploit, but did not dare to make the least Discovery of it to Mrs. *Brown*, who had very

justifiable

justifiable Reasons to reproach me for an Indiscretion she had prudently taken much Pains to prevent.

My first Design was to set forth in Pastry. 'Tis true I had an Oven, but not a single Penny to purchase a Faggot to light it, and for the Materials to make the Pies, they were equally uncomeatable But I took Courage, and went to inform the Widow Lady of my Intention, and entreat the Favour of her Custom.

As she is, without Compliment, a Person of Sense and Discernment, she very humourously asked me all the natural and necessary Questions, concerning the Motive and Means by which I was to settle myself, as she well knew I had not a Grain of the principal Ingredient towards exciting me to such a Resolution, or the effecting it

I confess I was strangely puzzled to answer her, and, after several Hums and Haws, told her, I hoped Fortune would favour my Design, as I only wanted to get an honest and decent Living, which was no small Recommendation to her Favour. After having smiled at my rash Undertaking, she administred

nistred that Kind of Comfort I stood most in need of at that Time.

To baking we went, and, partly through Pity and Curiosity, we took twenty Shillings the first Day. I then began to triumph greatly at my Success, and thought it my Turn to upbraid my Friend, for having reproached me for leaving the Stage.

I must not forget to insert a strong Desire I had to go to the Major, on the Strength of my Success, and hire a large Field of Grass, and, instead of a Bed, thought of purchasing a Horse, to carry Goods to the neighbouring Markets; but, that I might not appear more conspicuously ridiculous than I had done, Mrs *Brown* wisely dissuaded me from such a mad Scheme, and a few Weeks convinced me I had no Occasion for such a chargeable Conveyance of my Pastry. For, when every Body's Curiosity was satisfied, I found a terrible Declension of Business.

However, I met with unprecedented Friendships; especially from *Val----ne M----s*, Esq; who lives at *P------d*, a young Gentleman of a fair Character, and fine Estate. His Generosity enabled me to put the main Part of my Furniture into my House; and, as to
Linnen,

Linnen, and many necessary Materials besides, my good Friend, the young Lady before-mentioned, supplied me with them.

As I found one Business fall off, I resolved to set up another, and went, in one of my extraordinary Hurries, to buy a Sow with Pig, but, to my great Disappointment, after having kept it for near three Months, expecting it hourly to bring forth, it proved to be an old Barrow: And I, to make up the Measure of my prudent Management, after having put myself to double the Expence it cost me in the Purchase, was glad to sell it to a Butcher, for a Shilling or two less than I gave for it.

Thus ended my Notion of being a Hog-Merchant, and I having a Garden well stored with Fruits of all Sorts, made the best I could of that, 'till some villainous Wretches, in one Night's Time, robbed me of as much as would have yielded near three Guineas, besides barbarously tearing up the Trees by the Roots, and breaking the Branches through fearful Haste; being well assured, that the Gentleman who owned them would have punished them to the utmost Rigour of the Law, had they been discovered.

One Plague succeeding another, I resolved to leave the Place, and try my Fate in some other Spot, but, behold! we were run a little aground, so that we were positively oblig'd to sell the best Part of our Furniture to make up some Deficiencies, and we were once more in a bedless Condition.

With the necessary Utensils for the Pastry-Cook's Shop, and the friendly Assistance of some of our good Friends, we took Leave, and set out for a little Place, called *Pill*, a Sort of Harbour for Ships, five Miles of this Side of *Bristol*. The Place itself is not unpleasant, if it were inhabited with any other Kind of People than the Savages who infest it, and are only, in outward Form, distinguishable from Beasts of Prey. To be short, the Villainies of these Wretches are of so heinous and unlimitted a Nature, they render the Place so unlike any other Part of the habitable World, that I can compare it only to the Anti-Chamber of that Abode we are admonish'd to avoid in the next Life, by leading a good one here.

A Boy there of eight or ten Years of Age is as well versed in the most beastly Discourse and the more dreadful Sin of Blasphemy and
Swearing

Swearing, as any drunken Reprobate of thirty, and he who drinks hardest, and excels most in these terrible Qualifications, stands so most in his Father's Favour

There are some few that don't belong to the Boats, that are reasonable Creatures, and I am amazed they can patiently bear to reside, where there is such a numerous Set of Cannibals. A Name they very justly deserve, for, I believe, there are some among them, who would not scruple to make a Meal of their Fellow-Creatures.

I have seen many a suffering Wretch who has been Wind bound, sent away Half naked, after they had spent their ready Money, who have been obliged to strip themselves of their Cloaths, and glad to part from a Thing worth twenty Shillings to obtain, with Difficulty, one to keep them from starving, and that without any View of ever seeing it again. Nay, their Want of Principle and Christianity is such, that if they out-stay the Means of raising a Six-pence for a Bed, they will charitably turn them into the Street, to

" *Rest their Heads on what cold Stone they*
" *please.*"

For

For near six Months my Friend and I resided in this terrible Abode of Infamy and Guilt, but being ignorant, at our first coming, of what Kind of Mortals they were, we settled amongst them, and did not find it an easy Matter to remove, though we went trembling to Bed every Night, with dreadful Apprehensions of some ill Treatment before the Break of Day.

I took a little Shop, and because I was resolved to set off my Matters as grand as possible, I had a Board put over my Door, with this Inscription,

BROWN, PASTRY-COOK, FROM LONDON.

At which Place I can't charge myself with ever having, in the Course of my Life, attempted to spoil the Ingredients necessary in the Composition of a Tart. But that did not signify, as long as I was a *Londoner*, to be sure my Pastry must be good.

While the Ships were coming in from *Ireland* (which is in the Months of *June*, *July*, and *August*) I had a good running Trade, but, alas! the Winter was most terrible, and if an Uncle of my Friend's (who died

died while we were there) had not left her a Legacy, we must inevitably have perished.

About the Time the News came of her Money, we were involved to the Amount of about Four or Five and Thirty Shillings, and, if a Shilling would have saved us from total Destruction, we did not know where to raise it.

On the Receipt of the Letter I showed it to the Landlord, hoping he would lend me a Guinea to bear my Charges to Mrs. *Brown*'s Aunt, who lives in *Oxfordshire*, where I was to go to receive her Legacy, which was a genteel one, and I should have left her as a Hostage 'till my Return.

But the incredulous Blockhead conceived the Letter to be forged, and, as he himself was capable of such a Fraud, imagined we had artfully contrived to get a Guinea out of him, and reward him by running away in his Debt. But he was quite mistaken, as he was afterwards convinced, and made a Thousand aukward Excuses for his Unkindness when we received the Money, and had discharged his trifling Demands.

U I consulted

I confulted on my Pillow what was beft to be done, and communicated my Thoughts to my Friend, upon which we concluded, without fpeaking a Word to any Body, both to fet out and fetch the Money, according to Order, from her Relation's, though there was two very great Bars to fuch Progrefs, in the Eye of Reafon, but I ftepped over both

One was, having no more than a fingle Groat in the World between us. And the other, my having been obliged to pledge my Hat at *Briftol* a Fortnight before for Half a Crown, to carry on the anatomical Bufinefs, we haplefsly purfued.

Yet notwithftanding thefe terrible Difafters I was refolved, at all Events, to go the Journey. I took my Fellow-Sufferer with me, who was loft in Wonder at fo daring an Enterprize, to fet out, without either Hat or Money, fourfcore Miles on Foot. But I foon eafed the Anxiety of Mind fhe laboured under, by affuring her, that when we got to *Briftol* I would apply to a Friend, who would furnifh me with a fmall Matter to carry us on to *Bath*.

This

This pacified the poor Soul, who could scarce see her Way for Tears, before I told her my Design; which never entered my Imagination, 'till we had got two Miles beyond the detested Place we lived in. Our Circumstances were then so desperate, I thought

"*Whatever World we next were thrown*
    "*upon,*
"*Cou'd not be worse than* Pill"

As we were on our March, we were met by some of our unneighbourly Neighbours, who took Notice of my being in full Career, without a Hat; and of Mrs. *Brown*, with a Bundle in her Hand, which contained only a Change of Linnen for us, on our Travel.

They soon alarmed our Landlord with the Interview, with many Conjectures of our being gone off, and concluded, my being bareheaded was intended as a Blind for our Excursion. But let their Thoughts be what they would, we were safe in *Bristol* by the Time they got Home to make their political Report, and I obtained, at the first Word, the timely Assistance our Necessities required to procure a Supper and Bed that

Night, besides what served to bear our Charges to *Bath* next Morning.

The only Distress I had to overcome, was to procure a Covering for my unthinking Head, but Providence kindly directed us to a House where there was a young Journeyman, a Sort of a *Jemmy-Smart*, who dress'd entirely in Taste, that lodged where we lay that Night. As I appeared, barring the want of a Hat, as smart as himself in Dress, he entered into Conversation with me; and, finding him a good-natured Man, ventured (as I was urged by downright Necessity) to beg the Favour of him to lend me a Hat, which, by being very dusty, I was well assured had not been worn some Time, from which I conceived he would not be in a violent Hurry to have it restored, and, framing an Excuse of having sent my own to be dress'd, easily obtained the Boon.

Next Morning, at the Hour of Five, we set out, and staid at *Bath* 'till the Morning following. Though I remember I was obliged to give the Landlady my Waistcoat for the Payment of my Lodging before we went to Bed, which I had the Comfort of redeeming, by the Help of Mr. *Kennedy* and Company, and set forwards on my Journey with the Favour they were pleased to bestow on me.

I never received an Obligation in my Life that I was ashamed to acknowledge, though I have very lately incurred the Displeasure of a fine Lady, for mentioning a Person in my third Number, to whom I shall ever think myself most TRANSCENDANTLY OBLIGED, and shall never be persuaded to forget their Humanity, *or to reconcile Contradictions, and believe in Impossibilities.*

As soon as I was empowered, by the Help of a little Cash, we set out from *Bath* to *Oxfordshire*, and, in three Days, arrived at the happy Spot, where we were furnished with that Opiate for Grief, the want of which had many tedious Nights kept us waking.

Our Journey Home was expedited, by taking a Double-Horse from *Whitney* to *Cirencester*, and now and then, for the rest of the Way, mounting up into a Hay-Cart, or a timely Waggon.

When we returned to *Bristol*, we met with several of the *Pill* Gentry, who were surprized to see us, and informed us how

terribly

terribly we had been exploded, as being Cheats and Run-aways, and though they themselves, in our Absence, were as inveterate as the rest of the vulgar Crew, were the first to condemn others for a Fault they were equally guilty of.

I returned the borrowed Hat, and went Home triumphant in my own-----Paid my Landlord, and, as long as the Money lasted, was the worthiest Gentleman in the County, but when our Stock was exhausted, and we were reduced to a second Necessity of contracting a fresh Score, I was as much disregarded as a dead Cat, without the Remembrance of a single Virtue I was Master of, while I had a remaining Guinea in my Pocket.

Business daily decreasing, from the want of Shipping coming in, and the Winter growing fast upon us, we had no Prospect before us, but of dying by Inches with Cold and Hunger, and, what aggravated my own Distress, was having unfortunately drawn in my Friend to be a melancholly Partaker of my Sufferings.

This Reflection naturally rouzed me into an honourable Spirit of Resolution, not to let her perish through my unhappy and mistaken Conduct, which I meant all for the best, though it unfortunately proved otherwise, and, that I might not stay at *Pill* 'till we were past the Power of getting away, I sat down and wrote a little Tale, which filled up the first and second Columns of a News-Paper, and got a Friend to introduce me to Mr *W--- l*, Printer, on the *I----y*, who engaged me, at a small Pittance *per* Week, to write, and correct the Press, when Business was in a Hurry, which indeed it generally was, as he is a Man of Reputation, and greatly respected

I believe, if he had been perfectly assured who I was, and had known how much I had it in my Power to have been useful to him, as well as my self, it had been much better for us both. However, it was kind in him to employ a distressed Person, and a Stranger, to whom he could not possibly be under the least Obligation

Having secured something to piddle on, for I can call it no better, I ran back to *Pill*, to bless my Friend with the glad Tydings, and, as it was a long and dirty Walk from thence to *Bristol*, and infinitely dangerous over *Leigh-Down*, which is full

three

three Miles in Length, besides two miserable Miles before that to trudge, we thought it better to give up what we had to the Landlord, to whom we were but Eighteen Shillings indebted, though we left him as much as fairly stood us in Five Pounds ready Money, but, if we had offered to have made a Sale of it, I knew their Consciences would have given us Six-pence for that which might be worth a Crown or Ten Shillings. So we even locked up the Shop, and went with the Key in my Pocket to *Bristol*, and, in two Days Time, I sent it back with a Note, to let him know what we had left was entirely his own, for that we should never more return.

In Truth I have been as good as my Word, and shall continue so, for if Business or Inclination should ever excite me to take a Trip to *Ireland*, I would go *Chester* Way: And if Travellers knew as much as I do of that horrid Seat of Cruelty and Extortion, they would all come into the same Determination.

Having thus comfortably withdrawn ourselves from this hated Place, we took a Lodging at Two Shillings *per* Week; and, if I had not had the good Fortune to be kindly

kindly accepted on by a few Friends who were constantly inviting me, the remaining Part of my Wages would not have been sufficient to have afforded us, with other Expences, above two good Meals in a Week.

But Thanks to my Friends, who empower'd me to consign it all to the Use of one, to whom I should have thought, on this Occasion, if every Shilling had been a Guinea, I had made but a reasonable Acknowledgement, after having immers'd her in Difficulties which nothing but real Friendship and a tender Regard to my Health (which, through repeated Grievances, was much impaired) could have made her blindly inconsistent with her own Interest to give into, and so patiently endure.

This Business lasted for one Month exactly, and I found it impossible to subsist, without being troublesome to Friends; and Mr *W----d* not caring to enlarge my Income, I took it into my Head to try for a Benefit, and to that End printed some Bills in the Stile of an Advertisement, which were kindly presented to me by my Master.

All was to be done under the Rose, on Account of the Magistrates, who have not

suffered

suffered any Plays to be acted in the City for many Years, but notwithstanding I slily adventured to have *Barnwell* exhibited in the very Heart of it, at the *Black Raven*, in *High-Street*, where I had as many Promises as would have filled the Room (which was a large one) had it been twice as big. But, alas! they were but Promises, for instead of five and twenty Pounds, I had barely four, and abominably involved by the Bargain, insomuch, I was obliged to march quietly off, and say nothing.

After I was gone, several pitied my Misfortune, and declared, if I would make a second Attempt, I should be made Amends for the Disappointment of the former. But I thought it mighty well as it was, and, as I was safe in a whole Skin, would not run the Chance of being a second Time deceived, nor the Hazard of being more deeply engaged than I was.

I was so miserably put to my Shifts, that the Morning after my Malefit, I was obliged to strip my Friend of the ownly decent Gown she had, and pledged it to pay the Players, who came from *Wells* to assist me, which, to do them Justice, was a Difficulty they were entirely ignorant of.

'Twas

'Twas no small Mortification to me, not to have it in my Power to reward them genteelly for their Trouble; and more especially so, as my own Daughter was one of the Number, with her Husband, whom she imprudently married, contrary to my Inclination, about three Years before.

Though I had no Fortune to give her, without any Partiality, I look on her a more advantageous a Match for a discreet Man, than a Woman who might bring one, and confound it in unnecessary Expences, which I am certain *Kitty* will never do; and, had she met with as sober and reasonable a Creature as herself, in the few Years they have had a Company, might have been worth a comfortable Sum of Money, to have set them up in some creditable Business, that might have redounded more to their Quiet and Reputation

But I fear that is as impossible to hope or expect, as 'twould be likely to unmarry them; which, had it been in my Power, should have been done the first Moment I heard of the unpleasing Knot's being tied. But, as it is,

" *I here*

"I here do give him that with all my
"Heart,
"Which, but that he has already,
"With all my Heart I wou'd keep from
"him."

As my Child was at *Wells* with her Company, Nature was more prevalent in that Point than Necessity to fix me there, for there was another Set of People I could have gone to thirty Miles off, a different Road; but, notwithstanding my Dislike to her Marriage, I wanted to be as near her as I could, and joined them at *Wells*, where I was very well acquainted; and, as much as Players can expect, well regarded by the Best in the Town.

About three Years before, I had been there with Mr. *Elrington*'s Company, and we met with uncommon Success; but the last Time the Small-Pox raged violently there, and, if the Ladies and Gentlemen had not been extreamly kind, the poor Exhibiters might have been glad to have shared the Fate of the Invalids, to have been insured of a Repository for their Bones.

'Tis a common Observation, that Evils often produce good Effects, and such my Daughter

Daughter found from the Generosity of the Ladies, who made her several valuable Presents, which enlarged their Wardrobe considerably, and, being a well-behaved Girl, that recommended her to their Consideration, in respect of her private Character, and her publick Performance on the Stage, rendered her very pleasing to the Audience in general.

I humbly entreat to be believed, when, without Partiality, I aver her Genius would recommend her to a Station in either Theatre, if properly made use of, as she has an infinite Share of Humour, that calculates her for an excellent Low-Comedian, though she is obliged, having none equal to her Self, to appear in Characters in which her chief Merit consists in being positively a sensible Speaker.

I once saw her play *Horatia*, in *The Roman Father*, and was astonished to find her so truly affected with the Scene, where she comes to upbraid *Publius* for the Murder of her Lover, and provoke her own Death from her Brother's Hand. I confess I was pleasingly surprized, and beg Pardon for degenerating so far, as to speak in Praise of so near a Relation, who really deserved it, *An Error my Family is not very apt to run into*.

A second Time she gave me equal Delight in the Part of *Boadicea*, which I should never have suspected from her uncultivated Genius, but she proved she had one, in very justly acquitting herself in that Character, but yet I had rather see her in Low-Comedy, as 'tis more agreeable to her Figure, and entirely so to the Oddity of her humourous Disposition, and I wish she was so settled, as to constantly play in that Walk, which is a very pleasing one, and most useful when Players come towards the Decline of Life: For when they have out-lived the Bloom and Beauty of a Lady *Townly* or a *Monimia*, they may make very pleasing Figures in a Mrs. *Day* or a Widow *Lackit*.

I wish the Girl may take this friendly Hint, now she is young, as I am certain, in respect to her Years, she may, in all Probability, live long enough to make a considerable Figure in Characters of that Cast

I staid with her the Run of six Towns, the last but one of which was *Honiton*, in *Devonshire*, where I had the Happiness of gaining many Friends of Distinction; and perhaps should have continued longer, but that I

received

received a Letter from my Brother, to inform me, Mr. *Simpson* of *Bath*, had a Mind to engage me to prompt, and undertake the Care of the Stage, incidental to that Office.

As I was heartily tired of strolling, and being too frequently impertinently treated by my Daughter's Husband, I readily embraced the Offer, and set out for *Bath* with my Friend (who had been as often and equally insulted, by the little Insignificant) and on my Arrival, Mr. *Simpson*, in a Gentleman-like Manner, received me, and lent me a Sum of Money to equip me in my proper Character, which I repaid him Weekly out of my Salary, and thank him most sincerely for the Favour.

From the Month of *September* to *March* I continued there, but the Fatigue of the Place was more than my Health or Spirits could easily support; for, I am certain, the Prompters of either Theatres in *London* have not Half the Plague in six Months, that I have had in as many Days.

'Tis true Mr. *Simpson* was Owner, and ought to have been MASTER OF THE HOUSE; but his good Nature, and Unwillingness to offend the most trifling Performer, made him give up his Right of Authority, and rather stand neuter, when he ought to have exerted it.

The Hurry of Business in his Rooms, which were more methodically conducted than his Theatre, took up so much of his Time, 'twas impossible for him to pay a proper Attention to both. By this Means, what ought to have been a regular Government, was reduced to Anarchy and Uproar. Each had their several Wills; and but one, which was myself, bound to obey them all.

This any reasonable Person will allow to be a hard and difficult Task, as I was not inclined to offend any of them; and though they herded in Parties, I was resolved to be a Stranger to their Disputes 'till open Quarrels obliged me to become acquainted with them; and, in such Cases, I was often made use on as a Porter, to set these Matters to rights.

This, I confess, my Spirit could not easily brook; both in respect to my Father, as well as having been on a much better Footing, on a superior Theatre, than any I was obliged to pay a daily Attendance on.

I can

I can be upon Oath, during the whole Time of my Residence at *Bath*, I had not, even on *Sundays*, a Day I could call my own. And Mr *Bodely*, the Printer, can testify I have often left fresh Orders while he has been at Church, either for Alteration of Parts, or of Capital Distinctions in the Bills, without which very indifferent Actors would not otherwise go on.

I think 'twould have been a greater Proof of Judgment to have distinguished themselves on the Stage, than upon a Post or a Brick-wall, and I have often thought, when I have wrote the Word PERFORM'D, it would have been no Error to have changed it to DEFORM'D, of which I have often had melancholly Proofs from a Brace of Heroes, who, I believe, (one in particular) thought none equal to them. And truly I can't but be of their Minds, for two such GREAT MEN were never seen before, and, it is to be hoped, never will again.

As to the Women, the Principal, which is Miss *Ibbott*, is really deserving of Praise and Admiration, as all she does is from the Result of a very great and uncommon Genius. I own myself not very apt to be partial, but this

Gen-

Gentlewoman struck me into a most pleasing Astonishment, by her Performance of many Characters, but most particularly, in the Part of *Isabella*, in *The Fatal Marriage*. She not only drew the Audience into a most profound Attention, but absolutely into a general Flood of commiserating Tears; and blended Nature and Art so exquisitely well, that 'twas impossible not to feel her Sorrows, and bear the tenderest Part in her Affliction.

I must confess I never was more truly affected with a tragical Performance, and was rendered incapable of reading a single Syllable; but, luckily for Miss *Ibbott*, she is always so perfect, a Prompter is a useless Person while she is speaking. And it is no Compliment to insert what I told her when, she came off; that

------ "*Her whole Function suited*
"*With Forms to her Conceit*"

I am very certain there were several People of Quality down at *Bath*, who can testify the Truth of what I have said of her, and I should think it very well worth the while of the Masters of either of the Theatres to take her Merit into Consideration. And if she had the Advantage of seeing Mrs *Cibber*, Mrs *Woffington*, or Mrs. *Pritchard*, in their different

different Lights, it would make her as compleat an Actress as ever trod the *English* Stage.

The Merit of this Person was not a little conducive to the Interest of the Players in general, which was demonstrated in the Deficiency of the Nights Receipts whenever it happened that she was out of a Play, which indeed was very seldom. But as *Merit generally creates Envy, her Cotemporaries* would scarce allow it her, either publickly or privately, notwithstanding the politest Audiences testified it by a universal Applause, and they themselves proved it by the Odds of their Revenues, when first Characters have been *stuff'd up* by those who would have made better Figures as *her Attendants*, while she had PERFORM'D THEM.

The Business in general was, according to all Accounts, that Season better than they had known it for many past, and was greatly heightened by the universal Admiration of the Performance of the justly-celebrated Mr. *Maddox*, who engaged with Mr *Simpson* at a considerable Salary, though not more than he truly deserved.

I believe the Comedians found him worthy of his Income, as he not only brought in what paid his Agreement, but more than doubled that Sum, which they shared among them, yet, to my certain Knowledge, there was private Murmuring, even in respect to him, though they profitted by his Success, and, in spight of their grudging Hearts, could not help being delighted at his surprizing Feats of Activity on the Wire, which he is at *Whitsuntide* engaged to perform at Mr. *Hallam*'s Wells, in *Goodman's-Fields*, and intends to entertain the Town with several new Things, which he has never as yet publickly exhibited. I hope, not only in Respect to Mr. *Maddox*, but in Regard to Mr *Hallam*, who is an honest, worthy Man, he will be constantly visited by all People of true Taste.

Soon after Mr. *Maddox* left *Bath* (as Mr. *Fribble* says) a most terrible *Fracas* happened to the States-General of both the Theatres, occasioned by a mercenary View of Gain in an old Scoundrel, who was chiefly supported by charitable Donations; in which Mr *Simpson* (whose Humanity frequently prompts him to such Acts) had been often very liberal to this Viper, who rewarded him by lodging an Information against his, and the Company in *Orchard-Street*.

This

This put a Stop to the Business for about three Weeks, and was brought to a publick Process; but, I believe, an Attempt of the Kind will never be made again

As *Bath* is the Seat of Pleasure for the Healthful, and a Grand Restorative for the Sick, 'tis looked on as a Privileged-Place, and those who come only to please themselves expect a free Indulgence in that Point, as much as the Infirm do the Use of the Baths for their Infirmities, therefore a Suppression of any Part of their innocent Diversions was deemed, by the People of Quality, as the highest Affront that could be offered them, especially as they, and others of Distinction, are the absolute Supports of the Place; which, without them, would be but a melancholly Residence for the Inhabitants, if Custom had not made it fashionably popular, being a Town of no particular Trade.

This Reflection ought to put the strongest Guard upon them, not to be guilty of Offence themselves, or countenance it in others, which was positively the Case in Relation to this Affair, as it was proved a certain A------ raised a Contribution of twenty Guineas to
bribe

bribe the old Knave to put this cruel Design in Force against the Players.

This greatly exasperated every Person of Condition; who, as it was an Infringement upon their Liberty of Entertainment, interested themselves greatly in Behalf of each Theatre, and carried their Point against the insolent Invader of their Privileges.

During the Suspension, I could scarce walk through the Grove but the very Chairmen had something to say, by Way of Exultation, on the Misfortunes of the *poor Show-Folk*, as they impudently and ignorantly termed them, not considering that Play-Nights very greatly enlarged their Incomes.

Among this Set of *two-legged Horses*, were scattered some of the new-fangled methodical Tribe, who blessed their Stars that there was an End put to Prophanation and Riot.

'Tis surprizing that the Minds of those who wear the human Forms can be so monstrously infatuated, to be the constant Attendants on the canting Drones, whose Talents consist only in making a Shoe, or a Pair of Breeches.

Breeches. Have we not Thousands of fine Gentlemen, regularly bred at Universities, who understand the true System of Religion? And are not the Churches hourly open to all who please to go to them, instead of creeping into Holes and Corners, to hear much less than the Generality of the Auditors are able to inform their hypocritical Pastors?

I very lately visited Mr. *Yeates*'s New Wells, and was persecuted for an Hour with Words without Meaning, and Sound without Sense. I own, I should as soon think of dancing a Hornpipe in a Cathedral, as having the least Tincture of Devotion, where I had myself been honoured as a Heathen Deity, and dreaded as a roaring Devil.

No Mortal, but Mr. *Yeates*, could have thought of letting the Place for that Use; and, I believe, the first Symptoms of his Religion will be discovered, if there ever should be a Suppression of this Mockery of Godliness, in the Loss of his sanctified Tenants, and the sad Chance of the Tenement standing empty.

He must pardon me for this Liberty, but as we are both equally odd, in separate Lights,

neither

neither of us can ever be surprized or offended at what the other says or does.

My Warmth, I fear, has led me into an unnecessary Digression from my Story; but, I confess, I think the following these People so inconsistent with the Rules of Reason and Sense, I have not Patience to think that any Creature, who is capable of distinguishing between Right and Wrong, should listen to such Rhapsodies of Nonsense, which rather confounds than serves to improve their Understandings; and consequently, can be no Way instrumental to the Salvation of their Souls.

If publick Devotion, four Times a Day, is not sufficient for that Torrent of Goodness they would be thought to have, their private Prayers at Home, offered with Sincerity and Penitence, they may be assured will be graciously received, and prevent that Loss of Time bestowed in hearing the Gospel turned topsy-turvy by those, who really are as ignorant of it as the Rostrum they stand in, and whose Heads seem to be Branches of the same Root.

Notwithstanding the Gaiety of *Bath*, they swarm like Wasps in *June*, and have left
their

their Stings in the Minds of many. I am certain Rancour and Malice are particularly predominant in them, which they discovered in an eminent Degree when the Houses were shut up, by saying and doing all they could to have them remain so, to the Destruction of many Families, who were happy in a comfortable Subsistance arising from them.

I know 'twas some Guineas out of my Pocket, and though I grew heartily tired of my Office, I intended to have finished the Season, if this Disaster had not happened; but the Uncertainty of their Opening again, fixed in me a Resolution to leave them, which was strengthened by some ill-natured Rebuffs I had met with from the lower Part of the Company, which I scarce thought worth my Notice, having secretly determined to withdraw myself from that and the Fatigue, being, I think, more proper to be undertaken by a Man than a Woman.

One Thing I took monstrously ill, which I cannot help mentioning. Some Persons of Fashion, who had seen me in *London*, had a Mind that I should appear in the Part of Lord *Foppington*, in *The Careless Husband*, and, at their Request, I rehearsed it in a Visit, which they were so obliging to tell me, made them

them more anxious for my playing it. As a Proof that they defired it, they communicated their Defign to him *who ought to have been their Commander in Chief*, and he agreed to their Propofal, 'till two of his Subalterns, neither of which were qualified to appear in the Character, oppofed it; each hoping to fupply it themfelves, without the Advantage either of that Eafe in their Action neceffary to the Part, or being able to utter a Syllable of *French*. But what provoked me farther, was trumping up a Story of my Brother's having laid an Injunction on Mr *Simpfon*, never to permit me to go on the Stage, but particularly in that Character.

I believe the Town has had too many Proofs of my Brother's Merit, to fuppofe it poffible for me to be vain enough to conceive I fhould eclipfe it by my Performance, or that he was weak enough to fear it. And though I may be judged to have raifed my Thoughts to the higheft Pitch of Vanity, in believing that to be the real Cafe of my two Opponents in this Caufe, I am pofitively affured it was the main Motive of their being fo induftrioufly employed in preventing my coming on the Stage.

To fay Truth, I began to be very angry with myfelf for ever condefcending to fit behind

hind the Scenes to attend a Set of People, that, I was certain, whatever Faults I might have in Acting, not one of them, Miss *Ibbott* excepted, was capable of discerning.

The Intention of my Playing was framed by my Friends, to give me an Opportunity of recommending myself to a Benefit, who faithfully promised to exert their Interest for me; but their Scheme was soon frustrated, through the mean and dirty Artifice of these two People, who, I am certain, ought to endeavour at making every one their Friends, of which I have some modest Reasons to believe they frequently stand in need of.

Mr. *Falkner* very kindly offered to enter into the immediate Study of Lord *Morelove*, that the Play might not wait for him, and was pleased at a seeming Opportunity of my being more agreeably engaged than I was. But his good Nature is no Wonder, for I must do him the Justice to say I never heard him utter, or do a Thing, that was inconsistent with the true Character of a Gentleman.

This ill-natured Disappointment raised such Indignation and Contempt in me, that I as much abhorred to go to the House as some People do to undergo a Course of nauseous Physick;

Physick, but I soon removed myself, and, if they will forgive my ever having been there at all, I will promise them never to do so again.

Before I conclude the Account of my *Bath* Expedition, I cannot avoid taking Notice of a malicious Aspersion, thrown and fixed on me as a Reason for leaving it, which was, That I designed to forsake my Sex again, and that I positively was seen in the Street in Breeches

This I solemnly avow to be an impertinent Falshood, which was brought to *London* and spread itself, much to my Disadvantage, in my own Family, where I was informed it was delivered to them as a Reality, by an Actress that came to Town, soon after I quitted *Bath* I guess at the Person, but, as I know her to be half mad, must neither wonder or be angry at her Folly, yet, as she has sometimes Reason sufficient to distinguish between Truth and Falshood, am surprized she should meanly have recourse to the latter, to make me appear ridiculous, who never gave her the least Provocation to do me so apparent an Injury My only Reason for not staying, was an absolute Abhorrence to the Office I was in, and which I would not again undertake for Ten Guineas *per* Week

It

It happened, at the Time I left *Bath*, there was, without Exception, the most deplorable Set of *Non-Performers* at *Bradford* that ever wrecked the Heart of Tragedy, or committed Violence on the Ears of the Groundlings. I cannot say, with *Shakespear, They were Perriwig-pated Fellows*, for there was not a Wig and a Half throughout the whole Company, and, I believe, there was not above two Men that could boast of more than an equal Quantity of Shirts.

Business, they had none----Money, so long a Stranger to them, that they were in poor *Sharp*'s Condition, and had almost forgot the Current Coin of their own Country. With *these pleasing Prospects of Despair*, I joined their Community, and, as my Mind was unloaded from the Uneasiness I suffered from a Fund of impertinent Behaviour and everlasting Fatigue, greatly prejudicial to my Health, I sat quietly down, resolving not to repine at the worst that could happen, for the short Time I intended to stay with them.

A young Man at *Bath* had a Mind to indulge himself with a Mouthful of Tragedy, but, that he might have a Bellyful at once, gormandized the Part of *Othello*, which

brought

brought us a good House, and was a very seasonable Help, for we eat Our Landladies smiled, and we could call about us without the usual Tremor that had attended our Spirits for a Fortnight before, with the terrible Apprehensions of being answered with a Negative, or served with reproachful Doubts of their being ever paid.

A very few Days entirely broke up this disjointed Company, and we herded in Parties My Friend and I went with another Manager, almost as rich and wise as him we left, when, after having starved for two or three Towns, we received a very gross Affront, on which I went to the *Devizes*, where the above-mentioned notable Gentleman, with his Wife and a young Fellow, besides our two selves, made up the whole *Totte*.

They concluded we should play there, but rather than suffer an Insolence from such Mortals, even in the greatest Severity of Fortune, I rather chose to put myself to the utmost Inconveniencies I could possibly suffer As a Proof whereof, not having a Farthing in the World, I sold a few trifling Things for Four Shillings, and, with that scanty Sum, set out from the *Devizes* in *Wiltshire*, to *Rumsey*, in *Hampshire*, which, over *Salisbury-Plain bury-Plain*, is full forty Miles. But as there are no Houses over that long, solitary Walk, allowed to receive Travellers, we went under the *Plain* through all the Villages, which lengthened our Journey full twenty more.

Our Night's Expences, for Lodging and Supper, came to Nine-pence, so we positively had no more than Three Shillings and Three-pence to support us for sixty Miles.

My Friend, as she had great Cause, began, though in a tender Manner, to reproach me for having left *Bath*, and more especially, as Miss *Ibbott*, Mr *Falkner*, Mr *Giffard*, and many more, who came to see the *Comical Humours of the Moor of* Venice, *at* Bradford, used many forcible Arguments to make me return. Which I should have done, but that I happened to take Offence at something said to me on that Head by a particular Person, who notwithstanding I believe meant well, but being perhaps in a peevish Mood, as all the World at different Times are more or less, I persisted in my Resolution of not going back, and hope it will be no Affront to the theatrical Community at *Bath*, to assure them from my Heart, I never once repented it, but rather pitied my Successor for being encum-
bered

bered with a very fatiguing and unthankful Office.

When I set out from *Devizes*, I stood debating near an Hour on the Road, whether we should march for *London* or *Hampshire*, as our Finances were equally capable of serving us to either Place. But Nature asserted her Right of Empire in my Heart, and pointed me the Road to pay my Child a second Visit, and after a most deplorable, half-starving Journey, through intricate Roads and terrible Showers of Rain, in three Days Time, we arrived at *Rumsey*, having parted from our last Three Half-pence to ride five Miles in a Waggon, to the great Relief of our o'er-tired Legs.

It may be scarce believed that two People should travel so far upon so small a Pittance, who had not been from their Birth enured to Hardships; but we positively did, and, in the extream Heat of the Day, were often glad to have recourse to a clear Stream to quench our Thirst, after a tedious, painful March, not only to save our Money, but enable us to go through the Toil of the Day, 'till the friendly Inn received us, where our overwearied Spirits were lulled by Sleep into a Forgetfulness of Care.

I was

I was questioned, not long since, whether it was possible for me to have run through the strange Vicissitudes of Fortune I have given an Account of, which I solemnly declare I am ready to make Oath of the Truth of every Circumstance, and, if any particular Person or Persons require it, will refer them to Hundreds now living, who have been Witnesses of every Article contained in my History. Nor would I presume to impose a Falshood, where, as I was desired to give a real Account, Truth was so absolutely necessary, and, I believe, the Reader will find I have paid so strict a Regard to it, that I have rather painted my own ridiculous Follies in their most glaring Lights, than debarred the Reader the Pleasure of laughing at me, or proudly concealed the utmost Exigencies of my Fate: Both which may convince the World, that I have been faithful in my Declaration either Way; for none, I believe, desires, through *Frolick alone, to make Sport for others, or excite a Pity they never stood in need of.*

My Stay with my Daughter was but short, as I had made a considerable Progress in Mr. *Dumont*'s History, which, as I had determined not to lead that uncomfortable Kind of of Life any longer, I thought I could easily finish, during the weekly Publication, and frequently declared my Intention to my Daughter and her Husband, when I was at *Newport* in the *Isle of Wight*, with a positive Assurance that I would not go any farther with them.

This they either did not, or were not willing to believe, notwithstanding my frequent Repetition of it, and though I promised to make them happy with what might revert to me through my little Labours, they injudiciously conceived I was doing them an Injury, when, as I shall answer to Heaven, I intended it to turn equally to their Account as to my own: But a want of Understanding and good Mind on the one Part, and a too implicit Regard and Obedience on the other, led them both into an Error they had better have avoided

I would not have the World believe, notwithstanding my Aversion to the Choice my foolish Girl has made, that I would not, in all reasonable Respects, have every Action of her Life correspondent with the necessary Duty of a Wife, which, I am certain, never can or should exempt her from that she owes
me;

me, who must, while we both exist, be undoubtedly her Mother.

To be short, we parted; and, 'till I could turn myself about, I went with another of their Company (who left them, through Fears of the Small-Pox) to *Lymington*, where my Daughter enslaved herself for Life: From thence to *Fareham*, where, under a Pretence of bringing over some Hands to help us out, we being but six in Number, my Daughter's Spouse came only with a cruel Design to take away two of our Hands, in pure Spight to me; but, against his horrid Inclination, or Knowledge, he did me the greatest Piece of Service in the World, for I made a firm Resolution never more to set my Foot on a Country Stage

Since the pitiful Villainy of Strollers could reach one so nearly as one's own Blood, I thought it then high Time indeed to disclaim them. Though, I am well assured, the Girl would not have been guilty of the Crime of depriving her Mother of the Morsel of Bread she struggled for, had she not been enforced to it by a blind Obedience to an inconsiderable Fool.

I was monstrously ashamed to see an innocent Man, who was the Manager where I was then engaged, led into Difficulties, arising from an impudent Revenge on me I did not deserve, which the young Gentleman was too sensible of, and was not more concerned on his own, than my Account.

I prevailed on him to steer his Course to *London*, from whence, if his Affairs could have been properly adjusted, I absolutely intended to have returned for a short Time into the Country with him, from a Point of Gratitude and Honour, to make him in Part Amends for the Injuries he had sustained from my Son-in-Law, and I shall think he has an everlasting Claim, on that Score, to any Act of Friendship within my Power, whenever he thinks it consistent with his Interest to require it.

This good-natur'd, injur'd Person, had not only himself but a Wife and Child, exclusive of my unfortunate Phiz, to provide for, without the least Prospect of doing it, but, as I urged him so strenuously to go to *London*, I was determined to contrive the Means, and applied to a Friend of his, who very generously complied with the Request I made in his Behalf, and away we went for *Portsmouth*, hoping to have been Time enough for the Waggon which set out that Day.

We were unluckily too late, which obliged us to retard our Journey two Days, and remained at *Portsmouth* on Expences, which was a terrible Disaster, as our Finances were at best but slender. But had they been much worse, I was resolved to see *London*, by Heaven's Permission, if I had been obliged to have been passed to it, being worn out with the general Plagues of Disappointment and ill Usage, that are the certain Consequentials of a strolling Life.

When I set my Foot upon *London* Streets, though with only a single Penny in my Pocket, I was more transported with Joy, than for all the Height of Happiness I had, in former and at different Times, possessed.

I hope those who read the Description I have given of the Inquietudes that all must expect to meet with, who come under the impertinent Power of Travelling-Managers, will make a proper Use of it, by never forsaking a good Trade or Calling, of what Kind soever, to idle away their Lives so unprofitably to themselves,

themselves, and too often disadvantagiously to the Inhabitants of many an unsuccessful Town

I won't pretend to say, that all Heads of Companies are without a Rule of Exception, but, I must confess, those I have had to deal with, *and that very lately too, are what I have before described* And I doubt not but there are Numbers of my former Fellow-Sufferers, who are of my Opinion.

Thank Heaven, I have not, nor ever intend to have, any farther Commerce with them, but will apply myself closely to my Pen, and, if I can obtain the Honour and Favour of my Friends Company, at an Annual Benefit, I will, to the Extent of my Power, endeavour to entertain them with my own Performance, and provide the best I can to fill up the rest of the Characters.

I shall very shortly open my oratorical Academy, for the Instruction of those who have any Hopes, from Genius and Figure, of appearing on either of the *London* Stages, or *York, Norwich,* and *Bath,* all which are reputable; but will never advise or encourage any Person to make themselves VOLUNTARY VAGABONDS, for such not only the LAWS, but the Opinion of every reasonable Person, deems

deems those itinerant Gentry, who are daily guilty of the Massacre of dramatick Poetry. But of them, no more! but *a lasting, and long Farewel!*

When I first came to Town, I had no Design of giving any Account of my Life, farther than a trifling Sketch, introduced in the Preface to Mr DUMONT's History, the first Number of which will shortly make its Appearance, and I hope will be kindly received by my worthy Friends, who have favoured me in this Work, which I should never have undertaken, had I not been positively and strongly urged to it, not conceiving that any Action of my Life could claim that Attention I find it has, by the large Demand I have had for my weekly Numbers throughout *England* and *Wales*, for which I humbly offer my sincerest Thanks, and shall ever own myself not only indebted, but highly honoured.

As I propose my Pen to be partly my Support, I shall always endeavour to render it an Amusement to my Readers, as far as my Capacity extends, and, as the World is sensible I have no VIEW OF FORTUNE, but what I must, by HEAVEN'S ASSISTANCE, strike out of myself, I hope I shall find a Continuance of the Favour I at present am blessed with, and shall think it my Duty most carefully to preserve, not only in Regard to my own Interest, but from a grateful Respect to those who kindly confer it.

I entreat the Readers to excuse some Faults, which were Slips of the Press, occasioned through a Hurry of Business, that rendered it impossible to give Time for a proper Inspection, either by me or the Printer, who has been greatly hurried, on Account of the Benefits at both the Theatres, which he is indispensibly obliged to pay Regard to, in Point of Time.

'Tis generally the Rule to put the Summary of Books of this Kind at the Beginning, but as I have, through the whole Course of my Life, acted in Contradiction to all Points of Regularity, beg to be indulged in a whimsical Conclusion of my Narrative, by introducing that last, which I will allow should have been first. As for Example.

This Day, *April* 19, 1755, is published the Eighth and Last Number of *A Narrative of the Life of* Mrs CHARLOTTE CHARKE, with a Dedication from and to myself. *The properest Patroness I could have chosen, as I am* am most likely to be tenderly partial *to my poetical Errors, and will be as bounteous in the Reward as we may reasonably imagine my Merit may claim.*

This Work contains, 1*st*, A notable Promise of entertaining the Town with *The History of* HENRY DUMONT, *Esq*; *and Miss* CHARLOTTE EVELYN, but, being universally known to be an odd Product of Nature, was requested to postpone that, and give an Account of myself, from my Infancy to the present Time.

2*dly*, My natural Propensity to a Hat and Wig, in which, at the Age of four Years, I made a very considerable Figure in a Ditch, with several other succeeding mad Pranks. An Account of my Education at *Westminster*. *Why did not I make a better Use of so happy an Advantage!*

3*dly*, My extraordinary Skill in the Science of Physick, with a Recommendation of the necessary Use of Snails and Gooseberry Leaves, when Drugs and Chymical Preparations were not comeatable. My natural Aversion to a Needle and profound Respect for a Curry-Comb, in the Use of which I excelled *most young Ladies in* Great-Britain. My extensive Knowledge in
Gardening,

Gardening, not forgetting *that necessary Accomplishment for a young Gentlewoman*, in judiciously discharging a Blunderbuss or a Fowling-Piece. My own, and the lucky Escape of Life, when I run over a Child at Uxbridge.

4*tkly*, My indiscreetly plumping into the Sea of Matrimony and becoming a Wife, before I had the proper Understanding of a reasonable Child. An Account of my coming on the Stage. My uncommon Success there. *My Folly in leaving it.* My Recommendation of my Sister *Marples* to the Consideration of every Person who chuses to eat an elegant Meal, or chat away a few Moments with a humourous, good-natured, elderly Landlady. My turning Grocer, with some *wise Remarks* on the Rise and Fall of Sugars and Teas. An unfortunate Adventure, in selling a Link. A short Account of my Father and Mother's Courtship and Marriage.

5*thly*, A faithful Promise to prefer a Bill in *Chancery* against my Uncle's Widow, who has artfully deprived his Heirs at Law of a very considerable Fortune -----N B *The old Dame may be assured I will be as good as my Word*-----My keeping a grand Puppet-Shew, and losing as much Money by it as it cost

cost me. My becoming a Widow, and being afterwards privately married, *which, as it proved, I had better have let alone.* My going into Mens Cloaths, in which I continued many Years, the Reason of which I beg to be excused, as it concerns no Mortal *now living*, but myself. My becoming a second Time a Widow, which drew on me inexpressible Sorrows, that lasted upwards of twelve Years, and the unforeseen Turns of Providence, by which I was constantly extricated from them. An unfortunate Interview with a fair Lady, who would have made me Master of herself and Fortune, if I had been lucky enough to have been in Reality what I appeared.

6*thly*, My endeavouring at a Reconciliation with my Father. His sending back my Letter in a blank. His being too much governed by Humour, but more so by her whom Age cannot exempt from being *the Lively Limner of her own Face*, which she had better neglect a little, and pay Part of that Regard to what she ought to esteem THE NOBLER PART, and must have an Existance *when her painted Frame is reduced to Ashes.*

7*thly*, My being Gentleman to a certain Peer, after my Dismission, becoming *only an Occasional*

Occasional Player, while I was playing at *Bo-peep with the World.* My turning Pork-Merchant, broke, through the inhuman Appetite of a hungry Dog. Went a Strolling. Several Adventures, during my Peregrination. My Return, and setting up an Eating-House in *Drury-Lane*; undone again, by pilfering Lodgers. Turning Drawer, at St *Mary la-Bonne.* An Account of my Situation there. Going to the *Hay-Market* Theatre with my Brother. His leaving it. Many Distresses arising on that Account. Going a Strolling a second Time, and staying near nine Years. Several remarkable Occurrences, while I was Abroad, particularly, my being sent to G------ Jail, for being an Actor; which, to do *most Strolling-Players* Justice, they ought not to have the Laws enforced against them on that Score, *for a very substantial Reason.* My settling in *Wales*, and turning Pastry-Cook and Farmer. Made a small Mistake, in turning Hog-Merchant. Went to the Seat of Destruction, called *Pill.* Broke, and came away. Hired myself to a Printer at *Bristol*, to write and correct the Press. Made a short Stay there. Vagabondized again, and last *Christmas* returned to *London*, where I hope to remain as long as I live.

I have

I have now concluded my Narrative, from my Infancy to the Time of my returning to *London*, and, if those who do me the Honour to kill Time by the Perusal, will seriously reflect on the manifold Distresses I have suffered, they must think me wonderfully favoured by Providence, in the surprizing Turns of Fortune, which has often redeemed me from the devouring Jaws of total Destruction, when I have least expected it.

I WISH THE MERCIFUL EXAMPLE OF THE GREAT CREATOR, WHO NEVER YET FORSOOK ME, had prevailed on the Mind of him *who, by Divine Ordination, was the Author of my Being*, and am sorry that he should so o'er-shoot his Reason as not to consider, when I only asked for Blessing and Pardon, he should deny that which from a Superior Power *he will one Day find necessary himself to implore.* And I HOPE HIS PRAYER WILL BE ANSWERED, AND THAT HEAVEN WILL NOT BE DEAF TO HIM, AS HE HAS BEEN TO ME.

I cannot recollect any Crime I have been guilty of that is unpardonable, which the Denial of my Request may possibly make the World

World believe I have, but I dare challenge the moſt malicious Tongue of Slander to a Proof of that Kind, AS HEAVEN AND MY OWN CONSCIENCE CAN EQUALLY ACQUIT me of ever having deſerved that dreadful Sentence, OF NOT BEING FORGIVEN.

The Errors of my Youth chiefly conſiſted in a thoughtleſs Wildneſs, partly owing to having too much Will of my own in Infancy; which I allow was occaſioned by an over Fondneſs, *where I now unhappily find a fix'd Averſion* But notwithſtanding that Unkindneſs, Nature will aſſert her Right, and tenderly plead in the Behalf of him, who, I am certain, through Age and Infirmity, rather than a real Delight in Cruelty, has liſtned too much to an invidious Tongue, which had been more gracefully employed in HEALING, NOT WIDENING A BREACH BETWEEN A FATHER AND A CHILD, who wanted only the Satisfaction of knowing her Name was no longer hateful to him; who, in ſpight of Fortune's utmoſt Rigour, I muſt think myſelf bound, by all Laws both Divine and Human, *ſtill to cheriſh in my Heart and tenderly revere*

As I have nothing farther to entertain my Friends with, as to my Life, I ſhall, with the humbleſt

humblest Submission, take my Leave of them, and, as I design to pass in the *Catalogue of Authors*, will endeavour to produce something now and then to make them laugh, if possible, for I think 'tis Pity to draw Tears from those, WHO HAVE SO GENEROUSLY CONTRIBUTED TOWARDS MAKING ME SMILE.

FINIS.

Printed in the USA
CPSIA information can be obtained
at www.ICGtesting.com
CBHW081236111224
18822CB00012B/522